Luftwaffe Fledglings
1935-1945

Luftwaffe Training Units & their Aircraft

Barry Ketley & Mark Rolfe

HIKOKI
PUBLICATIONS

First published in Great Britain in 1996 by
Hikoki Publications
16 Newport Road, Aldershot, Hants, GU12 4PB

© 1996 Hikoki Publications

All rights reserved. Apart from any fair dealing for the purpose of private study, research, criticism or review, as permitted under the Copyright, Design and Patents Act 1988, no part of this publication may be reproduced, stored in a retrieval system, or transmitted in any form or by any means, electronic, electrical, chemical, mechanical, optical, photocopying, recording or otherwise, without prior written permission. All enquiries should be directed to the publisher.

ISBN 0 9519899 2 8

Except where credited otherwise, all photographs in this publication were provided via the author's collection

Edited by Barry Ketley
Colour Artwork by Mark Rolfe
Design by Hikoki Publications
Printed in Great Britain by
Martins the Printers, Berwick on Tweed

ALSO AVAILABLE
Hungarian Eagles 1920-1945
The Hungarian Air Forces 1920-1945
by
Gyula Sárhidai, György Punka & Viktor Kozlik
ISBN 0 9519899 1 X

Forever Farnborough
Flying the Limits 1904-1996
by
Peter J. Cooper AMRAeS
ISBN 0 951899 3 6

FORTHCOMING
**Royal Naval Air Service
1912-1918**
by
Bradley King
ISBN 0 951899 5 2

Eyes for the Phoenix
Allied Photo-reconnaissance Operations in South-east Asia in World War 2
by Geoff Thomas
ISBN 0 951899 4 4

Acknowledgments

The author expresses his thanks to all those who contributed photographs and Herren Schell and Munz of Albershausen in Germany for their help in supplying new primary reference material which has allowed the badge of FFS A/B 116 to be illustrated for the first time.

Publisher's note:

This small book is by no means exhaustive, but does represent the first serious attempt in English to tell the story of a fundamentally vital component of the Luftwaffe, previously almost totally neglected by historians and enthusiasts. Brief histories of the bulk of the aircrew training schools and units and their aircraft are given here. How they operated, where they operated and how, by mis-managing the training system, the Luftwaffe ultimately helped to destroy itself, demonstrates, if anything, how not *to run an air force. Strangely, despite the fact that so many Luftwaffe personnel went through these schools, little information is readily available concerning them, and the author would welcome any further information, pictures or comments. He can be reached via the publisher.*

Captions to front cover:

Focke-Wulf Fw 58C, used by the World War I naval ace, Friedrich Christiansen, in his capacity as Military Governor of the Netherlands. Previously Christiansen had been Korpsführer (leader) of the NSFK, and as shown here, decorated his aircraft with the same personal markings as used on his Hansa-Brandenburg W12 in 1917. The aircraft is known to wear a non-standard light blue colour scheme. Bearing in mind the individualistic Christiansen's previous links with both the navy and the NSFK, the aircraft is consequently shown in a blue close to the FAS 2 shade used on NSFK gliders

Lower: *Unit badges from left to right are: Bordfunkerschule Halle/Saale; A/B 43; A/B 1; LKS 7; LNS 6*

EAGLES IN THE NEST
Men, machines and methods

Until shortly before the official birth of the Luftwaffe on 1 March 1935, German air activity was totally geared to training – effectively there were no operational military aircraft. Forced to secrecy by the terms of the Armistice following World War I, the military aviation organisations which were formed in Germany could only function under the camouflage of civilian activities. This hampered the development of both aircraft and tactics, although it did provide for large numbers of aircrew who had been trained on a military basis. When the Luftwaffe sprang into being, fully formed as it were, the sudden appearance of squadron after squadron of fighters and bombers served as an apparently irresistible force which by and large deceived Hitler's potential enemies into acquiescing to his evermore strident political demands. The reality, however, was rather different; the years of subterfuge and economic constraint had taken their toll and, despite the Nazi propaganda of the time, German aircraft were neither as formidable nor as numerous as was claimed.

Adolf Hitler's opportunistic and expedient approach to politics led directly to the recognition by the military staffs that there would simply not be the time to build up forces in depth to sustain long campaigns before Germany found herself at war. In turn, this had great influence upon the development of the *Blitzkrieg* theory – massive and overwhelming strikes with all the forces available upon the key points of an opponent's armed forces which would rapidly overcome a numerically superior enemy. In this situation, therefore, it is easy to see how the requirements of a long term training plan could be subordinated to the short term need to use every available military asset, including reserves, in the first lightning assaults. Until the reverses in Russia this great gamble appeared to have paid off, but as soon as the war turned from one of rapid movement to one of steady attrition, thereby giving Germany's enemies time to re-arm and re-train, the failure to prepare for a long-drawn out struggle was, despite imaginative delaying stratagems, to prove terminal.

Training – the neglected necessity

After Munich Hitler had directed that the number of operational squadrons should be expanded fivefold. Given this overriding priority following on the reorganisation of the Luftwaffe General Staff in early 1939, the training element of the Luftwaffe, Branch 3, was restricted to tactical training in order to perfect the striking power of the new force. Longer term pilot training was handed over to the newly created office of Chief of Training, who reported directly to the Inspector General of the Luftwaffe, Erhard Milch. A further reorganisation

Above: Air-to-air view of an all-grey Arado Ar 66, RT+NX, in flight over the countryside somewhere near Bayreuth. Note how the letters on the fuselage have been painted over an earlier larger marking. The code letters have also been painted on the upper wing surface, a fairly uncommon practice (AMC)

of the Luftwaffe in April 1939 into what was to become a war footing led to the creation of *Luftflotten*, (Air Fleets), each occupying a specific area of the Reich.

From the beginning the relationship of the German training system to the operations structure was flawed. Incredibly, the Chief of Training did not control the training units. The commander of each Luftflotte was responsible for the training schools and equipment in his area. Naturally, the operational commanders were far more interested in the fighting force rather than the training system which only offered long term benefits. Following the outbreak of war, the pressing need to sustain the Blitzkrieg rapidly led the Luftflotte commanders to pluck the highly skilled flying instructors and their aircraft from the schools to serve as transport or courier units. Continued requisitioning of skilled instructors to meet the demands of a desperate shortage of transport aircraft led to a great weakening in both the quality and number of trained aircrew leaving the schools. From 1942, the effects of fuel shortages began to make themselves felt. Operational needs came first, and the training schools were at the end of a very long queue. Protests to the Luftwaffe Chief of Staff, *Generaloberst* Hans Jeschonnek, brought the reply "First we've got to beat Russia, then we can start training"!

Throughout its existence the Luftwaffe suffered from a high rate of landing and takeoff accidents, compounded by the natural tendency of young men to take risks. In the early days, the Luftwaffe was not as disciplined a force as might have been expected; over-confidence and showing-off led to many other, too often fatal, accidents. *Reichsmarschall* Göring referred to it as "a plague". Those who survived often became highly skilled through a combination of natural ability and the German system of war service which meant that aircrew could operate for years without ever being rested.

To an extent the failures of the training system were offset by the application of tactics which sometimes demonstrated a brilliant ability to improvise, but as the war progressed the pressures mounted. Shortages of equipment could be made up to a degree by expanding the number of production centres. Shortages of skilled personnel were not so easily rectified. It served little purpose to expand the number of training schools when to produce a good fighter pilot needed one year of training, and a bomber crew up to two.

During 1943 the training programmes were just about adequate, but by 1944, ironically just as aircraft production was reaching an all time high, the effectiveness of the pilots was falling hopelessly behind. By this time the average German fighter pilot was receiving about 160 hours of flying training before being hurled into action, while the opposing British and American pilots were completing about 360 and 400 respectively. Little wonder then that the losses amongst German pilots began to escalate rapidly. Lack of familiarity with their machines, lack of skill in flying in all weathers and a progressively increasing number of opponents led to an accelerating decline which was only to end in the final extinction of the once proud Luftwaffe.

The Men

Would-be aircrew recruits in the Luftwaffe quickly found out that the way to the stars required hard work. From 1935 onwards the usual precursor to the Luftwaffe was a preliminary period of road-building and ditch-digging with the paramilitary RAD *(Reichsarbeitdienst)* labour service. Alternatively, many of the more keenly air-minded opted for a period of training and indoctrination, which offered some basic flying training on gliders, with the NSFK *(Nationalsozialistisches Fliegerkorps)*, a civilian but Party-controlled organisation.

After induction into the Luftwaffe proper, all young recruits, including officer candidates and ground personnel, were sent to an FEA *(Fliegerersatzabteilung)*, later FAR *(Flieger-Ausbildungsregiment)*, for basic training in military discipline and physical culture lasting some 6-12 months. The only air aspects to be introduced would be in the form of lectures on radio and map-reading. Later in the war these courses would be abbreviated to 2 or 3 months only.

On passing out from the FAR, those recruits deemed to be suitable for flying training would be sent to a pool known as a *Fluganwaerterkompanie* for about 2 months where they studied general aeronautical subjects. Officer candidates would be sent to a *Luftkriegschule* (LKS).

At this point some explanation should be made of the various types of pilot licences issued by the Luftwaffe. Apart from the three grades of glider pilot licence issued by the NSFK, the basic powered aircraft A1 certificate required that the trainee complete a loop; three landings without an error; an altitude flight to 2000 m and a 300 km triangular flight course. All of these were to be accomplished in 1-2 seat aircraft weighing up to 500 kg.

A2 certification was similar except that it was for aircraft with at least two seats. Most pilots in the Luftwaffe trained on dual control machines, therefore this was the usual starter qualification. Following on from this was the B1 certificate. To obtain this the student had to show that he had already achieved at least 3000 km of flight experience; a 600 km triangular course in nine hours; an altitude flight to 4500 m and at least 50 flights in aircraft in the B1 category. (Singled engined 1-3 seater with a maximum weight of 2500 kg). On top of this experience, the pilot had to carry out three precision landings, two night landings and a night flight of at least 30 minutes.

2: Bücker Bü 131 at Heston. The Olympic rings on the cowling suggest that this is in summer 1936. Colour is probably silver overall with standard German markings of the period (Bruce Robertson)

3: Brrrr! Training carried on whatever the weather. Two overall RLM 02 Grau Bücker Bü 131 trainers warming up their engines on a snow-covered Luftwaffe training base. Both aircraft appear to carry codes beginning PE+??. Location may be in Czechoslovakia in winter 1939-40. Note that the machine on the left has the early style extended cranked engine exhaust

4: Unidentified Luftwaffe flight student running up the engine of RLM Grau 02 finished Bücker Bü 131, VT+AE or F, prior to a flight. Note the Bücker trademark between the cabane struts

5: The beginning of flight training. Bücker Bü 131, GD+ON, of FFS A/B 63 (note badge just below front cockpit). Marienbad 1941. FAR 63 was established on 1/12/38 at Eger. FFS A/B 8 was established in December 1939 in Marienbad. In February 1940, FAR 63 moved to Marienbad and took over A/B 8 in October 1940, at the same time taking the sitting tenant unit's number. Subsequently the school was renumbered FFS A/B 63 from 1/10/41. HQ at Marienbad, operations also from Karlsbad and Vilseck near Grafenwöhr.

6: Bücker Bü 131, one of the workhorses of the Luftwaffe primary flying training schools. In this case, KF+KT belongs to LKS 2 based at Reinsdorf near Jüterbog in 1942. (AMC)

7: Gefreiter Bruno Pacher seated in the cockpit of a Bücker Bü 131 discussing progress with his flying instructor, Feldwebel Tesch, on the ground. The original photo caption reads 'Landing after a training flight'. FFS A/B 8, Karlsbad 1941. (AMC)

The B2 certificate was progressively more difficult, requiring 6000 km of flight experience, including at least 3000 km on B1 class aircraft. In addition 50 further night flights were necessary, which had to include several difficult night landings.

To fly the larger multi-engined aircraft demanded the C licences. This required a minimum of 20,000 km flown in B-class aircraft (single-engined, 1-6 seats, weighing up to 2500 kg), 6000 km of which had to have been flown as first pilot. Not only this, the student had to complete a further 30 flights in C1 class aircraft (single-engined, 6 seats weighing over 2500 kg) and display a good general knowledge of aviation communications.

Ultimately, the most difficult certificate to acquire was the C2 which demanded the C1 licence as a prerequisite, plus an additional 30 training flights, several 800 km triangular flights, two flights on one engine only and a 200 km night flight.

From the above it is self-evident that good quality pilots, especially those flying the multi-engined bomber and transport types were not to be found quickly. Instructors capable of teaching up to these standards were even rarer, especially after the constant plundering of the training schools to supplement military operations. The shortage of qualified instructors led directly to inefficient training and a high wastage rate amongst the students, possibly as high as 25%.

However, back to the new student, who after being accepted for flight training would be posted to a *Flugzeugführerschule A/B* (FFS A/B) for 100 to 150 hours of primary training on A-2 and B-1/2 aircraft. At least, this was the theory – by the end of the war this was down to 40 hours, giving the teenage pilots little chance against the seasoned Allied flyers. The first 5 hours were dual, followed by another 25 hours or so practising circuits and bumps, takeoffs and landings and simple turns. Usual mounts for this were forgiving Bücker and Klemm types. As the trainee gained experience he was closely observed to establish what his aptitudes were, as these determined the next stage of training after he first gained his pilots' badge.

Prospective fighter pilots were passed on to a *Waffenschule* for 3 to 4 months where they carried out some 50 hours flying on different types, eventually leading to training on semi-obsolescent operational types. By the time he was posted to an operational squadron, still wet behind the ears, he would have flown for some 200 hours.

Dive bomber pilots were posted to the appropriate *Stuka Vorschule* for a course lasting 4 months during which they carried out about 15 dual practice dives before going solo. The physical strain imposed on the body during this limited the maximum number of solo dives permitted in a day to fifteen. Main purpose of the course was to achieve bombing accuracy; navigation and tactics were secondary.

Bomber and reconnaissance pilots were sent to *FFS (C)* schools where the training was on twin-engined aircraft. Lasting from 3 to 6 months, the course allowed for about 60 hours of flying by day and night, including cross-country and some blind flying. On completion of this stage on obsolescent types, the pilot went for a further six weeks to a specialist *Blindflugschule* where there would another 50-60 hours of blind-flying practice. The final stage was about three months at a specialist bomber or reconnaissance school where complete crews were trained on current operational aircraft types. Having passed through some 250 hours flying during a course lasting anything between 18 months to 2 years, the crews were eventually posted to an operational squadron.

The special requirements of marine pilots demanded a rather different approach insofar as their training, right up to 'C' certificate level, usually took place at the same base. Consequently a much larger variety of aircraft could be seen at the *Flugzeugführerschulen (See)*.

A glaring omission from this training schedule is that for transport pilots. The preoccupation of the Luftwaffe High Command with offensive i.e. bombing, operations caused them to grossly underestimate the logistics needs of modern warfare and to begrudge using aircraft for transport and supply purposes. Compounded by a failure to appreciate the vulnerability of such aircraft to enemy action, the result was that apart from having to remove skilled instructors from the flying schools, until 1943 transport units were classified as *Kampfgeschwader zur besonderen Verwendung (KGzbV)* – literally 'Bomber Unit on Special Duties'!

One other aspect of aircrew training should be mentioned here. In a direct link with the conventions of the First World War, the observer of a German bomber was to be the captain of the aircraft, the pilot being a mere chauffeur. Consequently, the observer had to be the most experienced member of the crew and capable of taking over the duties of other members in an emergency. His training was therefore both varied and comprehensive. Trained up to 'C' certificate standard as a pilot with 150 hours under his belt, he then attended a special observers school for intensive training in navigation, night and blind-flying, bomb-aiming, radio operation and gunnery! Needless to say, the pressures of war soon brought about a reassessment of the duties of these paragons, and from 1942 onwards the amount of training an observer received began to decline. His status as aircraft captain was also removed and eventually a 4-6 month course was the norm.

As previously noted, once war began, training for the Luftwaffe began to fragment. Relatively efficient and well organised at the beginning, the system was geared specifically to the needs of short sharp campaigns. Experience of the rasp of war quickly led to modifications. For instance it was soon recognised that there was a need for further training in tactics and familiarisation with the particular type of aircraft and unit the pilot was to be posted to. The result was the formation of numerous *Erganzungsgruppen* (Operational Training Schools) which were linked to operational units, and numerous ad hoc specialist training courses such as anti-shipping. A major omission had been night fighting, which most definitely required specialist training, and typified the lack of foresight shown by the High Command, while the development of new aircraft, weapons and tactics led to further proliferation.

The Elementary Flying Units

Prior to the outbreak of World War 2 the disguised training units went through the usual bewildering relocations and redesignations so typical of the birth pangs of the Luftwaffe. With the expansion of the Reich territories, a considerable number of the schools were moved east into newly occupied countries. Eventually, by September 1939, there were some 50 A/B schools in existence, many of which shared the same bases as the related FAR training regiments. (At this point it is worth noting that the flying schools frequently occupied more than one airfield. For example, A/B 8, based in Czechoslovakia, used fields at Marienbad, Vilseck and Karlsbad). Subsequently, as fortune turned against Germany, many were merged to form *Doppelschulen* or were closed prior to the general collapse of the training system in 1943-44. The list which follows includes brief details of all the more important schools known at the present time. *Table 1.*

Table 1

Luftwaffe Elementary Flying Training Schools

School	Date Formed	Main Bases Used	Comments
FFS A/B 1	January 1940	Görlitz	A1 from October 1943
FFS B1		Schweinfurt	
FFS A/B 2	September 1939	Magdeburg-Ost, Deblin-Irena	Became A/B 21
FFS A/B 2		Luxeuil, Strasbourg	New formation. May 1942 became A/B 120. Closed 1944
FFS A/B 3	September 1939	Guben	Became A3. September 1943 joined with A/B 113
FFS A/B 4	September 1939	Prague/Gbell	To Neudorf/Oppeln July 1941
FFS A/B 5	October 1939	Seerappen	March 1941 merged with A/B 33.
FFS A 5	1944	Gablingen	Closed February 1945
FFS A/B 6	November 1936	Danzig-Langfuhr	Renamed Sch/FAR 52 June 1941
FFS A/B 7	October 1939	Plauen/Chemnitz	
FFS A 7	February 1944	Schweinfurt	Operational until January 1945
FFS A/B 8	December 1939	Marienbad/Vilseck	Became Sch/ FAR 63 October 1940.
FFS A/B 9	December 1939	Grottkau/Stephansdorf	February 1944 with A32 formed Doppelschule A 9.
FFS A/B 10	November 1938	Neukuhren	Merged with A/B 125 May 1940.
FFS A/B 10	June 1940	Warnemnde/Volkenshagen	Reformed. From October 1943, A10.
FFS A/B 11	November 1938	Schönwalde	August 1943 with A/B 125 at Neukuhren to become A 125.
FFS A/B 12	November 1939	Königsberg/Neumark Halberstadt/Stargard	May 1943 to Prenzlau as A 12.
FFS A 12	December 1943	Prenzlau/Pasewalk	With A 71. Closed February 1945.
FFS A/B 13	November 1939	Pilsen, Neubiberg	From April 1943 at Neubiberg
FFS A/B 14	December 1938	Klagenfurt/Aigen	Closed November 1944.
FFS A/B 21	January 1940	Magdeburg-Ost, Deblin-Irena	June 1941 to Luxeuil, then split, part going to Metz to form A/B 124.
FFS A/B 22	August 1939	Neustadt/Parchim	
FFS A/B 23	November 1939	Kaufbeuren	Operational till end of war.
FFS A/B 24	October 1939	Parndorf, Olomouc	February 1943 to Kitzingen with A/B 121 as A 121.
FFS A/B 31	January 1940	Posen/Schroda	
FFS A/B 32	October 1939	Pardubitz	February 1944 to Grottkau with A/B 9 as A 9.

Table 1

Luftwaffe Elementary Flying Training Schools

School	Date Formed	Main Bases Used	Comments
FFS A/B 33	December 1938	Darmstadt, Königsberg	From January 1941 at Quakenbück. July 1942 to Altenburg. May 1943 became BFS 10.
FFS A/B 41	?	Frankfurt/Oder	Operational until January 1945
FFS A/B 42	September 1939	Prenzlau/Ückermark	September 1940 to Neustadt-Glewe. September 1942 to Langensalza. September 1943 to Helmstedt. Closed November 1944.
FFS A/B 43	March 1939	Crailsheim/Böblingen Deiningen, Niederstetten, Nellingen, Nuremburg.	From October 1943 with A/B 124 as A 43. Closed January 1945
FFS A/B 51	January 1940	Heiligenbeil	December 1941 to Elbing. February 1943 became FFS C1.
FFS A/B 52	August 1940	Halberstadt/Wernigerode	Danzig-Langenfuhr 1940. As A/B 6 from June 1941. January 1945 at Celle.
FFS A/B 53	December 1938	Platting	Merged with A/B 5 during working up.
FFS A/B 61	February 1939	Oschatz, Werder/Havel	From May 1944 as A 61. Closed December 1944.
FFS A/B 62	November 1939	Bad Vöslau/Trausdorf	July 1943 became JG 108.
FFS A/B 63	December 1938	Marienbad/Eger	A/B 8 from October 1940 until October 1941, when it became A/B 63 once again.
FFS A/B 71	May 1940	Prossnitz/Stichowitz	December 1943 to Prenzlau with FFS A/B 12 to form Doppelschule A12.
FFS A/B 72	November 1939	Markersdorf-St. Pölten, Fels/Wagram	Formed at Detmold. June 1944 to Schwerin-G rries. Closed September 1944.
FFS A/B 82	November 1939	Cottbus, Pretsch	October 1941 to Pretsch.
FFS A/B 110	Late 1939	Stubendorf	June 1943 became BFS 11.
FFS A/B 111	Late 1939	Oels, Roth	March 1941 to Roth. February 1942 became FFS(C) 13.
FFS A/B 112	Late 1939	Tulln, Ingolstadt, Böblingen	With LKS 7. October 1941 to Böblingen. August 1943 to Nellingen as A112.
FFS A 112	August 1943	Nellingen	Closed December 1944.
FFS A/B 113	March 1940	Brünn/Mähren	September 1943 joined by A/B 3 to form Doppelschule A 3.
FFS A/B 114	Late 1939	Zwölfaxing-Wien, Weimar-Nohra	July 1943 to Weimar. February 1945 became A 114.
FFS A/B 115	Late 1939	Wels	Dissolved as A 115 in March 1945.
FFS A/B 116	Late 1939	Neudorf-Oppeln, Göppingen	June 1941 to Göppingen. Closed October 1944.
FFS A/B 117	February 1940	Kamenz, Bad Aibling	July 1941 probably closed.
FFS A/B 118	February 1940	Stettin-Altdamm, Braunschweig-Broitzen	To Braunschweig-Broitzen in December 1944. Closed March 1945.
FFS A/B 118	February 1940	Stettin-Altdamm, Braunschweig-Broitzen	To Braunschweig-Broitzen in December 1944. Closed March 1945.
FFS A/B 119	February 1940	Jüterbog-Damm, Kassel-Rothwesten	To Kassel summer 1941. Closed May 1943.
FFS A/B 120	Summer 1940	Prenzlau/Uckermark, Luxeuil	May 1942 moved to Luxeuil (France), merged with FFS A/B 2.
FFS A/B 121	Summer 1940	Straubing	June 1943 joined by A/B 24 to form Doppelschule A 121. End 1944 became LKS 1. Limited operations until January 1945.

Table 1
Luftwaffe Elementary Flying Training Schools

School	Date Formed	Main Bases Used	Comments
FFS A/B 122	?	Gütenfeld, Jena-Rödigen/Rockau	September 1940 at Gütenfeld. April 1941 to Jena. Unknown after July 1942.
FFS A/B 123	July 1941	Agram (Zagreb), Graz-Thalerhof	Trained Croat personnel. May 1943 moved to Graz as A 123. Closed September 1944.
FFS A/B 124	June 1941	Metz-Diedenhofen, Metz-Frescaty	October/November 1943 to Crailsheim where merged with A/B 43 to form A 43.
FFS A/B 125	June 1941	Neukuhren, Elbing, Prowehren, Lyck.	August 1943 absorbed A/B 11 to form Doppelschule A 125. July 1944 to Fassberg, December 1944 to Parow.
FFS A/B 126	June 1941	Gotha	Not known after June 1942.
FFS (See) 1	1933	Warnemünde (Breitling)	Began life as DVS Warnemünde in 1925, close to the Heinkel factory. Dispersed in January 1941
FFS (See) 2	April 1936	Pütnitz	Renamed FFS (C) 17 in January 1941 as a land-based unit.
FFS (See) 3	1934	Stettin	Founded as DVS Stettin. Became FFS in October 1939 until end 1940, then probably absorbed by A/B 118.

The Machines

At the time of the declaration of the existence of the Luftwaffe in 1935, the training aircraft in use ranged from single seat gliders to heavy aircraft weighing over 2500 kg. These were classified with Germanic thoroughness into different groups which corresponded to the different pilot certificates. With just a few exceptions the civilian registrations carried by these land-based aircraft served to identify the class, as shown in *Table 2*.

As previously noted, there were a few well chosen anomalies within the system. With the Nazis' well-developed taste for subterfuge, those aircraft carrying registrations beginning D-I were "experimental". In reality these were most often military aircraft, and frequently not even seaplanes. An example is an Heinkel He 45, registered D-ISES which was in service as a reconnaissance aircraft with Aufklärungsgruppe 24 based at Kassel-Rothwesten

Table 2
German Civilian Aircraft Classifications & Registrations
1935

Class	Personnel	All-up Weight	Engines	Registration Group
A1	1-2	Up to 500 kg	1	D-YAAA to D-YZZZ
A2	1-3	Up to 1000 kg	1	D-EAAA to D-EZZZ
B1	1-3	Up to 2500 kg	1	D-JAAA to D-JZZZ
B2	4-6	Up to 2500 kg	1	D-OAAA to D-OZZZ
C1	6	Over 2500 kg	1	D-UAAA to D-UZZZ
C2	6	Over 2500 kg	2+	D-AAAA to D-AZZZ

Classifications for marine aircraft were similar except for weight differences as below:

Class	Personnel	All-up Weight	Engines	Registration Group
A1	1-2	Up to 600 kg	1	D-YAAA to D-YZZZ
A2	1-3	Up to 2200 kg	1	D-EAAA to D-EZZZ
B	1-4	Up to 5000 kg	1	D-IAAA to D-IZZZ
C	6	Over 5500 kg	2+	D-AAAA to D-AZZZ

Table 3		German Aircraft Classifications 1944	
Class	Personnel	Land-based	Marine types
A1	1	Up to 500 kg	Up to 600 kg
A2	1-3	500 to 1000 kg	600 to 2200 kg
B1	1-4	1000 to 2000 kg	2200 to 5500 kg
B2	1-8	2500 to 5000 kg	2200 to 5500 kg
C	Varied	Over 5000 kg	Over 5500 kg

during 1935. With the development of more sophisticated and inevitably heavier machines, the classifications were changed several times during the war. By 1944 they looked like *Table 3*. By the summer of 1939, the OKL (High Command of the Luftwaffe) and the RLM (Reich Air Ministry) had agreed upon a basic establishment of aircraft for the A/B schools. In theory each A2 school was to have 45 aircraft, B1 schools to have 21 and the B2 schools to have 30. Logically one would assume that this would have been accompanied by a rationalisation of the numerous different types of trainers then in use with consequent advantages in production and maintenance. Rationalisation would have also made it easier to regulate standards of training. Nevertheless, in a manner typical of the neglect attending the training services, the question of rationalisation was not seriously addressed until October 1944 – far too late to be more than an academic exercise.

The overwhelming need for the German aircraft industry to produce combat aircraft meant that production of new trainer aircraft was slow, in many cases taking place in occupied countries, primarily Czechoslovakia and France. Apart from the sometimes dubious quality of the final product, with liberation these production centres were lost, creating yet more pressure upon the training system. In most cases training schools were forced to function with a bewildering variety of machines, including captured enemy aircraft, in a bid to stay operational. An indication of the diversity of machines in use for primary and basic training in the early war years is given in *Table 4*.

Table 4

A2 Land: Bü 131, Bü 133, Bü 181, Fw 44, He 72, Kl 25, Kl 35

B1 Land: Ar 65, Ar 66, Ar 68, Ar 76, Ar 96, Fw 56, Go 145, He 45, He 46, He 51, Bf 108

B1 Sea: He 42W, He 60W, He 114

B2 Land: Fw 58, He 70, Ju F13

B2 Sea: Ju W33 W, Ju W34 W

In addition, odd examples of obsolete types such as the Albatros L101 survived to carry the swastika. Later still in the war the need for specialist trainer versions of combat aircraft was belatedly recognised and this led to production of two-seat versions of the Focke-Wulf Fw 190, Messerschmitt Bf 109 and Messerschmitt Me 262.

Apart from the German produced types there were many captured aircraft to be seen on Luftwaffe training airfields. Prominent among these were Czech Praga and Avia machines. Numerous examples of the US-built North American NA 57, (the fixed undercarriage predecessor of the Texan), which had been in service with the Armée de l'Air in France, were also used. In addition, many French fighters were utilised as advanced trainers, particularly the Dewoitine D.520. Generally speaking, any reasonable captured enemy aircraft could find itself in the Luftwaffe training inventory, even some Soviet designed machines such as the Tupolev SB-2 (FFS (C)2 being one known user) were found useful employment. A good indication of the range of exotic types used by the Luftwaffe can be found in an RLM order dated 16 March 1943 which listed types to be scrapped or withdrawn from service. These included a number of ex-civilian models, some in service in extremely limited numbers. *Table 5*.

It is not possible to list every aircraft type ever used in the A/B schools here, but brief descriptions of all the major machines designed for primary and basic training

Table 5

Zlin XII	Airspeed Envoy
Zlin 212	Puss Moth
Beneš-Mráz Be 51	Tiger Moth
Aero 100	Moth Major
Morane-Saulnier MS 230	Leopard Moth
Caudron 635	Gloster Gladiator
Fokker G 1	Vega Gull
PWS 26	Caproni Ca 135
RWD 8	Tipsy B

German types also to be withdrawn:
Bücker Bü 180	Arado Ar 95
Bücker Bü 182	Arado Ar 195
Blohm & Voss Bv 141	Arado Ar 231
Junkers Ju 46	Dornier Do 17J,R,S,V

follow, roughly in the order in which a student might encounter them. Data refers to the main production versions.

Klemm Kl 25

A small two-seater open cockpit monoplane produced by Klemm Leichtflugzeugbau GmbH at Böblingen. Of rugged all-wood construction, with a fixed spatted undercarriage, the first examples flew in 1928 powered by 20 hp Mercedes engines. Later versions used a variety of engines, both in-line and radial, of progressively greater power. Fifteen were exported to Britain before the war where they used several different British engines, including the 75 hp Pobjoy R. Another 28 were built under licence in Britain by the British Klemm Aeroplane Co. as the B.A. Swallow. Some 600 were built in Germany between 1929-1935 and saw service with all the different Nazi paramilitary flying training organisations such as the DVS, DLV, NSFK and Luftdienst as well as the Luftwaffe. Used on float and ski undercarriages as well as wheels, they were not particularly aerobatic; their 13 m wingspan gave them admirable gliding characteristics, which however made them prone to 'float' on landing, to the discomfiture of many a student pilot. At least one, D-ENAA, survived until the end of the war to be captured at Stuttgart-Echterdingen by the American 324th Fighter Group, still in its original pre-war silver finish!

Span:	13.00 m/ 42 ft 7 3/4 in
Length:	7.50 m/ 24 ft 7 1/4 in (L 25d VIIR with Hirth HM 60R engine)
Weight:	720 kg/1587 lb (Fully loaded)
Max Speed:	160 kmh/100 mph

Klemm Kl 35

Probably the most important product of the Klemm company, the Kl 35 was a rather more elegant gull-winged younger brother to the L25. Designed for the private owner, like the rest of the Klemm stable, the fixed undercarriage Kl 35 first flew in 1935 powered by an Hirth HM 60R in-line engine of 80 hp. Built both with and without enclosed cockpits, the Kl 35 was constructed from wood with a combination wood and fabric covering, substantial numbers were produced as the Kl 35A and Kl 35AW floatplane with the Hirth 60R engine. With the 105 hp Hirth HM 504A engine it was known as the Kl 35B and Kl 35BW floatplane. Three of the landplane models served with a pre-war Lithuanian Aviation Platoon (*Lietuvoje Šauliu Sajungos*).

In 1938 the Kl 35D flew, powered by a 105 hp Hirth HM 504A-2 engine and with a strengthened undercarriage which could also be fitted with skis or floats. This was destined to be the main production version, about 3000 being built and intended from the outset for service as a Luftwaffe trainer, subsequently seeing considerable service throughout World War 2. Several were exported to Hungary and Romania. Twenty-five were purchased by the Slovak air force. After importing several Kl 35B and D types, the Swedes acquired a production licence in 1941-42 to build about 74 examples of the Kl 35D for use by the *Flygvapnet*, some of which served until 1951.

Span:	10.40 m/ 34 ft 1 1/2 in
Length:	7.50 m/ 24 ft 7 1/4 in
Weight:	750 kg/1653 lb (Fully loaded)
Max Speed:	210 kmh/130 mph

Bücker Bü 131 *Jungmann*

Bücker Flugzeugbau was founded in 1932 at Berlin-Johannisthal, and quickly established itself as a major supplier of training aircraft to the embryonic Luftwaffe. Jointly designed by Carl Clemens Bücker and his Swedish chief design engineer, Anders Andersson, the Bücker Bü 131 was the first product from the company and flew for the first time in 1934. A neat but conventional biplane, (the last such type to be built in Germany) the Bü 131 had two open tandem cockpits and a fixed, sprung undercarriage. Construction was a combination of rugged steel tubing for the fuselage and tail covered with a mixture of metal and fabric, while the wings were fabric covered wood. Powered by the popular Hirth HM 60R inline engine of 80 hp, early deliveries of the B 131A went to the paramilitary DLV (*Deutscher Luftsportverband*), forerunner of the Luftwaffe. In 1936, the Bü 131B, powered by the 105 hp Hirth HM 504A-2 engine began to enter service with the elementary flying training schools of the Luftwaffe. In service with virtually all the A/B schools throughout World War 2, although in declining numbers as training and obsolescence took their toll, the need for aircraft to equip hastily-formed night ground-attack squadrons led to many a Jungmann donning warpaint. Prominent amongst these *Nachtschlacht Gruppen* were NSGr 2, formed in 1942 and NSGr 11 and 12 in Estonia and Latvia, manned by crews from those countries.

Equally successful in the primary training role in other countries, 315 examples found their way to the air force of Hungary, while Czechoslovakia built 10 under licence as the Tatra T 131 before the war. Most wartime versions for the Luftwaffe were later produced by Aero in Prague. One of the most important pre-war customers was Jugoslavia, to where as many as 400 may have found their way. Pro-Axis users also included Bulgaria (15) and Rumania (40). CASA in Spain licence-built a further 530 or so, while Switzerland standardised their training on the Bü 131 and used 94, 88 of which were licence-built by Dornier. 1037 examples with Japanese *Hatsukaze* engines were built for the Imperial Japanese Army Air Force as the Kokusai Ki 86, and a further 339 for the Imperial

8: Bücker Bü 133C, D-EQOA, being flown by Rudolf Lochner, the 1937 German Aerobatic Champion during a demonstration over the Rangsdorf Lake in 1937. The aircraft is finished in the early standard factory finish of pearl white paint on all wood and fabric surfaces, with silver-finished metal panels and engine cowling (Bruce Robertson)

9: A Bücker Bü 181 in a most unusual RLM 02 Grau overall finish. This is probably one of the earliest production models, as almost all the production versions of the Bestmannn were finished with dark green uppersurfaces (Bruce Robertson)

10: Student pilot climbing into a Bü 181, ??+KW, possibly belonging to LKS 2 at Berlin-Gatow. Note the netting separating the luggage compartment from the cabin

Japanese Navy as the Kyushu K9W1 *'Cypress'*, as their standard primary trainer. Another Oriental user was the ML-KNIL in the Dutch East Indies with just one Bü 131.

Many Swiss and Spanish examples still fly today, albeit with more modern engine, while in an astonishing rebirth, 1994 saw work commence on twenty new-build Jungmann and Jungmeister by Büker Prado SL in Spain. These used CASA jigs and some original parts, when they were known as the BP 131 and BP 133.

Span: 7.40 m/ 24 ft 3 in
Length: 6.62 m/ 21 ft 8 1/2 in
Weight: 680 kg/1500 lb (Fully loaded)
Max Speed: 183 kmh/114 mph

Bücker Bü 133 *Jungmeister*

The success of the company's Bü 131 naturally led to a logical development for more advanced training. The result was the Bü 133, a single seat aerobatic and advanced trainer, which used many components from the Bü 131 but in a slightly smaller airframe. Flown for the first time in 1935, incidentally by German's first woman works pilot, Luise Hoffmann, the prototype Bü 133 V1, D-EVEO, was powered by a Hirth HM 506 in-line engine of 140 hp. Demonstrated publicly for the first time at the International Aerobatic Championships in Rangsdorf in 1936, the astonishing agility of the little biplane quickly attracted the attention of the leading aerobatic pilots of the day. No production of the Bü 133A followed, and two aircraft only with 160 hp Siemens-Bramo Sh-14A radial engines known as the Bü 133B were built, before being superseded by the main production version, the Bü 133C. Powered by the same engine as the previous model, but with a distinctive helmeted cowling and a 13 cm shorter fuselage, the outstanding flying qualities of the Bü 133C

soon led to a string of aerobatic championship wins. By 1938 the Jungmeister had become the standard aerobatic trainer of the NSFK and Luftwaffe. A three-man aerobatic team drawn from the Luftwaffe was so impressive at Brussels in 1938 that Göring ordered that a nine-aircraft team be formed. This made a tremendous impression when it appeared at the International Flying meeting at Brussels in July 1939. Unfortunately, the Luftwaffe's display team was to have only a brief existence before the

11 Above: View to port from the front seat of a Focke-Wulf Fw 44 as it sits on the flight line with two others. The next aircraft, ??+BM, has an unusual style of lettering

12 Left: Air-to-air shot of Focke-Wulf Fw 44F, DD+CP, Werk Nummer 24 (?) of FFS A/B 13, in flight over Pilsen, Czechoslovakia, 1940

outbreak of war in September that year. The quality of the basic design was such that about fifty Bü 133A and Bü 133C machines were built under licence in Spain. A further 52 Bü 133Cs were also licence-built by Dornier in Switzerland as the standard Swiss Air Force aerobatic trainer, where they remained in service until 1968. The Jungmeister was so good that it was a genuinely competitive aerobatic aircraft until well into the 1960's!

Span:	6.60 m/ 21 ft 8 in
Length:	6.02 m/ 19 ft 9 in
Weight:	585 kg/1290 lb (Fully loaded)
Max Speed:	220 kmh/137 mph

Bücker Bü 181 *Bestmann*

The outstandingly successful biplanes produced by the company did not blind Bücker to modern developments, and the next design was a neat high-wing monoplane, the Bü 134, inspired by the American Piper Cub. D-EQPA, the sole example, flew in 1936 but did not prove to possess particularly pleasant handling. Not only this, but by then the German lightplane market was firmly enamoured with the low-wing monoplane concept. Consequently, the next design, the Bü 180 *Student*, was of this configuration. With tandem seating for two people the Bü 180 pioneered new construction techniques for Bücker, comprising all-wooden wing structure and a steel tube, metal covered forward fuselage with a wooden monocoque aft. About 20 were built, both with and without cockpit canopies, before wartime conditions forced a halt to production. At least two, however, coded PF+WQ and PF+WR, found their way to A/B 8 in Marienbad during April-May 1941.

Derived from the Bü 180, the single-seat Bü 182 *Kornett*, preceded the Bü 181 into limited production. Intended for military training, the little Bü 182 flew in late 1938, but as the RLM displayed little interest only three more were completed before the design was abandoned in favour of a two-seat cabin trainer. Built in direct response to an urgent RLM request for such an aircraft, the result was Bücker's last and most modern design, the Bü 181.

Originally designed for sports and touring use, the Bestmann largely replaced the earlier Bücker designs in Luftwaffe service. Following the same general constructional principles established by the Bü 180, the undercarriage was a sturdy fixed cantilever type with single legs. The cabin offered side-by-side seating for two with a capacious baggage compartment behind. The first prototype, D-ERBV, flew in early 1939 and the superb flying qualities displayed by the aircraft led quickly to its selection as the Luftwaffe's latest (and last) primary trainer. First deliveries of the Bü 181A, powered by a 105 hp Hirth HM 504 engine, began in late 1940. Demand for the new trainer was such that the factory in Rangsdorf was unable to cope. As a result, the Fokker company in Holland was allocated the task. Beginning in 1942, 718 examples of the Bü 181A and slightly modified Bü 181D were produced there. Most aircraft served with the Luftwaffe, although 24 were delivered to the Hungarian Air Force from 1942 onwards. Swedish experience with the earlier B cker types led to the licence-building of 121 examples of the Bü 181B as the Sk 25, while the Czech Zlin factory commenced manufacture just before the end of the war. Many more were produced there post-war under the Zlin label. There were even licence-built versions of the Zlin in Egypt. Total wartime production, including 180 from the Zlin plant, was several thousand.

In a desperate attempt to halt the flood of Allied armour roaming across Germany in early 1945, a number of provisional anti-tank squadrons, manned by volunteers and equipped with Bü 181s jury-rigged with *Panzerfaust* anti-tank rockets under the wings, were formed. One

13: Near miss for the pilot of Fw 44, D-EVYM, (possibly Werk N. 345), who has narrowly escaped being eaten by an Argus-engined He 72. Note the blue fuselage spine to the nearest aircraft. The lucky pilot appears to have had a personal accident! The finish of the aircraft indicates that these machines were actually being operated by the DLV, predecessor to the Luftwaffe (AMC)

aircraft in particular, coded PU+BN, had previously belonged to FFS A/B 14 in Klagenfurt. These *Panzerjagdstaffeln* saw action near Kaufbeuren, Grossenbrode, Magdeburg and Berlin. In almost every case the result was the loss of both aircraft and pilot. Several of these machines later defected to Switzerland and six subsequently served with the Swiss *Fliegertruppe* until 1956.

Span:	10.60 m/ 34 ft 9 in
Length:	7.85 m/ 25 ft 9 in
Weight:	750 kg/1650 lb (Fully loaded)
Max Speed:	215 kmh/133 mph

Focke-Wulf Fw 44 *Stieglitz* (Goldfinch)

Under the leadership of the legendary Kurt Tank, the first really successful aircraft from the Focke-Wulf company flew in late summer 1932. Known as the Fw 44, a neat radial-engined biplane seating two people in tandem open cockpits, the design displayed numerous faults. Extensive testing and redesign, led by Tank, eventually eradicated these and the result was a sturdy machine with excellent flying characteristics. A conventional enough single-bay biplane constructed with a steel tube fabric covered fuselage and wooden wings, also fabric covered, whose most distinctive visual feature was probably the large streamlined fairings to the fixed undercarriage legs. The first small production batch, known as the Fw 44E, was powered by a 120 hp Argus in-line engine, but the bulk of the machines built were of the Fw 44F type. These were powered by the reliable Siemens Sh 14a radial engine.

Aerobatic pilots of the calibre of Ernst Udet and Gerd Achgelis quickly helped establish a reputation for both the aircraft and the manufacturer. The result was a massive influx of orders, which established Focke-Wulf Flugzeugbau GmbH as a major aircraft manufacturer. Before the war the Stieglitz formed the initial equipment of many of the early DVS, DLV and Luftwaffe units. In service in large numbers throughout the war with many of the A/B schools, several examples survived until the 1950's. Apart from overseas buyers in Bolivia, Chile, China, Czechoslovakia, Finland, Romania, and Switzerland, five countries produced the type under licence, namely: Austria, Argentina, Bulgaria, Brazil and Sweden.

Span:	9.00 m/ 29 ft 6 1/4 in
Length:	7.30 m/ 23 ft 11 3/8 in
Weight:	870 kg/1919 lb (Fully loaded)
Max Speed:	185 kmh/115 mph

Heinkel He 72 *Kadett* (Cadet)

Another of the numerous two-seat German sports and training biplanes of the 30's, the prototype Heinkel He 72A, D-2574, first flew in 1933 and was powered by a 140 hp Argus As 8B in-line engine. A totally conventional biplane of fabric-covered metal construction, with tandem seats in open cockpits, machines of this type equipped several NSFK units. After a short production run of He 72A's, most aircraft were built with the more powerful 160 hp Siemens Sh 14A radial engine, which often made it difficult to distinguish from the similarly powered Fw 44. In this configuration it was known as the He 72B and subsequently saw service at many Luftwaffe training schools. A single experimental example with floats was built, the He 72BW, but was not proceeded with; the earlier and bigger He 42 was considered to be more efficient in this role. 30 He 72B-3 *Edelkadetts* with spats over the mainwheels were built for civilian use. Final development of the He 72 family was the sole He 172, D-EEHU, which differed mainly in the use of a cowling for the Siemens engine.

Robust, but with performance verging on the modest side, the He 72 seems to have been overshadowed by the more modern Bücker types, yet it had its moment of glory when ex-Slovak Air Force examples were used by the Slovak insurgent combined squadron for reconnaissance during the abortive uprising at Tri-Duby in summer 1944.

Span:	9.00 m/ 29 ft 6 1/4 in
Length:	7.50 m/ 24 ft 7 1/4 in
Weight:	865 kg/1907 lb (Fully loaded)
Max Speed:	185 kmh/115 mph

Arado Ar 66

One of the half-dozen or so small biplane types used as primary trainers by the Luftwaffe, the Ar 66 followed a similar formula of fabric-covered mixed wood and metal construction. An entirely conventional trainer, probably the most notable difference between the Ar 66 and other trainers was the use of a distinctive Arado shaped rudder without a fin. First flown from Arado's Warnemünde factory in 1932, the prototype Ar 66a was powered by an Argus As 10C inline engine of 240 hp. An essentially similar second landplane prototype was preceded by the Ar 66b floatplane which was fitted with twin floats attached to numerous struts. Ten of these were produced as the Ar 66B in 1933 but failed to find favour and did not reach operational service. Main production of what was to become the Luftwaffe's most numerous, yet paradoxically, probably least well known landplane primary trainer, began in 1933 as the Ar 66C. Powered by the same Argus As 10C engine as the prototypes, the Ar 66C was assigned to most of the A/B schools and performed well in steady, if unspectacular, fashion.

14: Closeup of the cockpits in the wreckage of Focke-Wulf Fw 44F, DD+CR, from FFS A/B 13 at Pilsen, Czechoslovakia. Note the dark green finish, the white outlined black letters and the barely legible name, 'Marieanne' at an angle on the fuselage just in front of the cabane strut. Giving names to training aircraft was a very rare practice in the Luftwaffe – or any other airforce for that matter. Both occupants of the aircraft apparently escaped serious injury

15: Front three-quarter view of one of the rarer versions of the Focke-Wulf Fw 44 elementary trainer; the Fw 44E, powered by an in-line Argus engine. Variants fitted with this engine were known in the Luftwaffe as the 'Zitter-Stieglitz' – Shaky Stieglitz! PS+NG, (possibly WNr 376), was serving with FFS A/B 13 based at Pilsen, Czechoslovakia, 1940

16: A typically assorted lineup of Luftwaffe training aircraft. From right to left: Focke-Wulf Fw 44, Bücker Bü 131, Praga E39 coded SA+?V, Praga E39, three Fw 44's. The unit and location is not positively identified, but is believed to be A/B 9 at Grottkau

17: Pristine Focke-Wulf Fw 44's of an unknown unit. The nearest machine, Werk Nummer 233, appears to carry a fuselage code beginning with SD

18: Two examples of the Focke-Wulf Fw 44F, workhorse of the Luftwaffe primary flying training schools. PT+NF, Werk Nummer 2554, in service with FFS A/B 13, carries an overall grey finish and a yellow fuselage band and is seen at Pilsen, Czechoslovakia, sometime between 1940 and April 1943 when the school transferred to Neubiberg

19: Starboard side view of Focke-Wulf Fw 44F, BO+CM, being restrained by ground crew shortly before beginning its take-off run. Unit and location may be A/B 9 at Grottkau

The unpleasant and irritating nocturnal activities of Soviet Polikarpov U-2 biplanes on the Eastern Front prompted the Germans to respond in kind. After casting about for a suitable vehicle, large numbers of sturdy and tractable Ar 66C and Go 145 trainers were selected to see action. Formed initially into *Störkampfstaffeln* (Night-harassing squadrons), these aircraft were reorganised in late 1943 into *Nachtschlacht Gruppen* (Night GroundAttack Groups), where they saw extensive service behind the Russian frontlines dropping booby-traps and light anti-personnel bombs. Some 2000 Ar 66 trainers were modified for this role with underwing bomb racks and operated on dark nights at treetop level, often wearing ski undercarriages. Sixteen Staffeln were formed using these aircraft, including one manned by Estonians, two by Latvians and one by Russian volunteers.

Span: 10.00 m/ 32 ft 9 3/4 in
Length: 8.30 m/ 27 ft 2 3/4 in
Weight: 1330 kg/2933 lb (Fully loaded)
Max Speed: 210 kmh/130 mph

Arado Ar 76

Originally designed as a lightweight single-seat advanced fighter-trainer capable of being used as an 'emergency home defence fighter' in response to a request from the still-secret RLM in 1934, the Ar 76 was just one of four designs considered for the purpose. Competing proposals were also prepared by Focke-Wulf, Henschel and Heinkel. The specification indicated a marked preference for a monoplane to be powered by the Argus As 10C liquid-cooled engine and with an armament of two 7.9 mm MG 17 machine guns and three 10 kg bombs in the fighter role. As a trainer the only armament required was a single MG 17.

Arado's prototype was a strongly built parasol with a simple tubular steel fuselage with a covering of alloy and fabric, while the wings were constructed from fabric-covered wood. The elegant but heavy little machine had provision for the two required guns in the classic nose position, with a small bay just behind the engine to hold three bombs. D-ISEN, the first prototype, was lost early in the test programme and was followed by two other prototypes which had modified tail surfaces. In the evaluation of the competing designs, Focke-Wulf's Fw 56 Stösser gained first place, although the Ar 76 came such a close second that a small production batch of the Ar 76A was ordered as a backup. These were delivered to the Luftwaffe as trainers in the spring of 1936. Known users included FFS A/B 8, FFS A/B 23 and LKS 1 at Kamenz.

Span: 10.88 m/ 35 ft 8 1/2 in
Length: 10.30 m/ 33 ft 9 1/2 in
Weight: 2125 kg/4684 lb (Fully loaded)
Max Speed: 349 kmh/217 mph

Arado Ar 96

Far and away the most important advanced trainer in the Luftwaffe inventory, the Ar 96, designed by Dipl. Ing. Walter Blume (a First World War *Pour le Mérite* holder), was an extremely advanced aircraft when it first flew in 1938. D-IRUU, the Ar 96 V1, was a very clean low-wing monoplane of all-metal construction with tandem seats for instructor and pupil beneath a fully glazed canopy and an outwards retracting undercarriage. Powerplant was the popular Argus As 10C inline engine. A distinguishing feature was the typical tall Arado fin and rudder assembly. Apart from changing the undercarriage to an inwards retracting type to better withstand the rough handling by ham-fisted pupils, the type was accepted for production with little change. A small batch of Ar 96A-1's was completed in 1939, but were felt to be underpowered and consequently the Ar 96B, powered by the Argus As 410 engine of 465 hp and with a lengthened fuselage to accommodate more fuel, became the main production variant. First deliveries from the Arado and AGO factories joined the training schools in summer 1940. The Ar 96B-1 was unarmed; the B-2 and B-3 series carried a single MG 17 in the starboard upper engine cowling; the B-5 was also fitted with FuG 16ZY VHF radio; the B-6 tested underwing bomb racks and resulted in the B-7 production version. There was no B-4. A single machine was tried out with a single MG 15 on a flexible mounting in the rear cockpit, while a small pre-production batch fitted with a small belly window for bomb-aiming practice and a 480 hp Argus engine was known as the Ar 96C.

Much of the early Ar 96 production was carried out in the AGO plant, but from mid-1941 the Avia company in Prague took over. Avia was joined by the Letov factory from late 1943 and the two completed the bulk of the 11,546 machines built. The Czechs continued production of the Ar 96 as the C-2 until 1949.

Apart from the A/B schools, thirteen *Jagdschulgeschwader* (fighter-training wings) eventually used the Ar 96, as well as the fighter replacement units (*Erganzungjagdgruppen* – EJG) and the officer cadet schools (*Luftkriegschulen* – LKS).

The qualities of the Ar 96 naturally recommended it to Germany's allies, consequently 65 Ar 96A's and 45 Ar 96B's were used by the *Magyar Királyi Honéd Légierő* (Royal Hungarian Air Force). One example of the Ar 96B was also licence built by the Hungarian MÁVAG concern. A single Ar 96A and three Ar 96B types were also used by the Slovak Air Force *(Slovensk Vzdušné Zbraně)*.

Span: 11.00 m/ 36 ft 1 in
Length: 9.13 m/ 29 ft 11 1/4 in
Weight: 1695 kg/3747 lb (Fully loaded)
Max Speed: 330 kmh/205 mph

Focke-Wulf Fw 56 *Stösser* (Falcon)

Winner of the 1934 RLM competition for a 'home-defence fighter', the agile little Fw 56 was the first design for the Focke-Wulf Flugzeugbau which was totally supervised by the talented Kurt Tank. First flown in November 1933, the incorrectly registered prototype, D-JSOT, was a neat parasol monoplane, not dissimilar to the competing Ar 76. Considerable attention was paid to aerodynamic cleanliness in order to squeeze maximum performance out of the 240 hp Argus As 10C engine with which it was powered. Entirely conventional in structure, with a steel-tube fuselage covered by fabric and a similarly covered wooden wing, the design was steadily refined through the next four prototypes, V2-V5. An abbreviated faired-in fin and curved rudder gave a clue to the Albatros ancestry of the type. (Albatros and Focke-Wulf had merged in 1931). During testing, several problems were encountered with the undercarriage and strength of the wing. These were eventually resolved and led to the distinctive backward raked single-strut undercarriage legs and an amazing diving ability. Ultimately, the final competition was held in summer 1935 where the Fw 56, in the shape of the V6, alias A-03, D-IXYO, was judged to be the winner. Neither as aerobatic nor as fast as the Ar 76 or the He 74, the Stösser won on account of its strength and handling which were similar to the new monoplane fighters such as the Messerschmitt Bf 109.

Ordered into production as the Fw 56A-1, the machine entered service with the Luftwaffe fighter schools fitted with one or two MG 17 machine guns. When in service with the NSFK no armament was fitted. As befits an advanced fighter-trainer, until mastered it could be something of a handful for trainee pilots, but when in the hands of a skilled pilot it was a delightful machine. By the time production ended in 1940 about 1000 examples had been built. These saw extensive service with both the fighter schools and a number of experimental establishments, where it was instrumental in the development of the Mistel piggy-back concept. A very few found their way into service with initial training schools, known users being FFS A/B 41 at Frankfurt am Oder and FFS A/B 112 at Langenlebarn/Tulln.

In 1937, export orders for the Fw 56 were permitted and the result was a small batch of 12 for the Austrian *Luftstreitkäfte*. It was not long, however, before these were in service with the Luftwaffe following the *Anschluss* in March 1938. The Hungarians were also attracted by the Stösser and purchased 32 examples between 1937-39.

Span:	10.50 m/ 34 ft 5 1/2 in
Length:	7.60 m/ 25 ft 3 1/4 in
Weight:	996 kg/2196 lb (Fully loaded)
Max Speed:	278 kmh/173 mph

Gotha Go 145

First product of the Gothaer Waggonfabrik AG following its resurrection in 1933, the Go 145 was a contemporary of the several other primary training biplanes of the new Luftwaffe. Designed by Dipl. Ing. Albert Kalkert, the Go 145 followed standard practice of the time by being an open-cockpit two-seat biplane of wood and fabric construction with the customary 240 hp Argus As 10C inverted-vee engine. The fixed undercarriage and two-bladed propeller were also standard features of the period. One little-known feature, however, did set the Go 145 apart from other trainers – namely that with the exception of the Go 145 – student pilots sat in the rear cockpit.

Following the first flight of the prototype in February 1934, large orders were placed for the Go 145A production version. These rapidly established a reputation for durability and pleasant handling and soon equipped almost half the A/B schools. Throughout the war, demand for the type was so great that it was also built by AGO, Focke-Wulf and BFW. At least 9,965 were built in Germany, while CASA in Spain and Demag in Turkey also built about 1000 between them for service in their own air forces. The Spanish versions remained in service until long after the war.

An experimental version with enclosed canopies known as the Go 145B appeared in 1935 but did not enter service, while another, the Go 145C, with an MG 15 gun in the rear cockpit was used in small numbers for gunnery training.

After the arrival in force of Soviet night harassing biplanes during 1942, the Go 145 was chosen, in concert with the Ar 66, to be the main equipment of the German counter-squadrons. Scores of Go 145's fitted with a selection of guns, bombs, loudspeakers or even rockets roamed over the entire Eastern Front at night. The outdated biplanes proved to be so successful in the hands of the 13 *Störkampfstaffeln* (harassing squadrons) that by October 1943 they were redesignated as *Nachtslachtgeschwader* (night attack groups) and many were still in front-line service in May 1945.

Although the activities of the Go 145 have gone largely unrecorded, the type did much to establish Gotha as one of the foremost wooden aircraft builders in Germany, which culminated in them being given responsibility for building the futuristic Horten Ho 229 flying wing jet fighter-bomber in 1945.

Span:	9.00 m/ 29 ft 6 1/4 in
Length:	8.70 m/ 28 ft 6 1/2 in
Weight:	1380 kg/3043 lb (Fully loaded)
Max Speed:	212 kmh/132 mph

20: A line of Heinkel He 42B training floatplanes drawn up on the slipway at Warnemünde, possibly being used by Flieger Schule 2, Travemünde, 16 July - 30 September 1935. D-2033, the nearest machine was first registered in April 1931 to the DVS, one of the many cover organisations used in the establishment of the clandestine Luftwaffe. Several survived until 1944. This machine certainly survived until at least 1934. Note the small winged 'H' Heinkel trademark on the fin (AMC)

21: A view into the rear cockpit of an Heinkel He 72C

22: A captured Klemm L 25, D-ENAA, which survived the war to be captured by the American 324th Fighter Group at Stuttgart-Echterdingen. Finished overall silver, the aircraft probably once belonged to the NSFK

23: *Snow did not hold up training. Close view of the forward fuselage of a Klemm L25 with another on skis taking off in the background. Large numbers of these Klemm trainers saw service with FFS A/B 8, flying from the field at Marienbad during winter 1940/41 – code letters for at least seventeen are known. The cross flag marks the assembly point for waiting students (AMC)*

24: *Air to ground picture of an all-grey Klemm Kl 35, NQ+??, being flown solo as it passes over the cameraman. The parent unit may be A/B 9 at Grottkau*

25: *Starboard side view of a Klemm Kl 35, KC+BR (or B/P?) of FFS A/B 33 at Elbing in 1940 (AMC)*

Heinkel He 42

Mainstay of the three Flugzeugführerschulen (See), the first prototype, Werk No. 333, of this robust single-engined two-seat floatplane (then known as the HD 42) first left the water off Warnemünde on 3 March 1931. An entirely conventional fabric covered biplane based on Heinkel's extensive experience with marine aircraft, the prototype proved to require little modification and a first batch of 32, known as the He 42A, was completed in 1932. Powered by the uncommon Junkers L-5 300 hp engine, experience with these led to a new version, the He 42B-0, which used a more powerful Junkers L-5-G engine. Two of the ten B-0 versions built were modified by Heinkel as part of a programme of strengthening to suit the machines for catapult launching. Additionally fitted with new radio, these modified B-0s became the first of 36 B-1s intended for sea reconnaissance. Incorporating various further minor improvements, the final versions, the He 42C-1 and C-2 differed mainly in the provision of a single machine gun for the C-2 to better fit it for overwater reconnaissance. The C-1 was a dedicated unarmed trainer with a slightly less powerful engine. Both types survived as trainers until about 1944, although late in their career many were also used as target tugs by the navy.

Span:	14.00 m/ 45 ft 11 in
Length:	10.60 m/ 34 ft 10 in
Weight:	2420 kg/5336 lb (Fully loaded)
Max Speed:	200 kmh/124 mph

26: Closeup view of the nose of a gull-winged Klemm Kl 35 trainer carrying the short-lived 'WL' code, which was officially used by Luftwaffe training aircraft for less than a year, between January to October 1939. Note how crowded the registration appears where the fuselage cross has been crammed in between the letters. The picture is believed to have been taken at Grottkau, where the aircraft was in service with A/B 9, sometime in 1940

27: Two Klemm Kl 35 trainers of LKS 2 await the next flight. The location is probably Güterfelde near Potsdam, sometime in 1942. The aircraft in the background appears to carry an exceptionally wide yellow fuselage band which extends out to the vertical bar of the letter 'E'

28: *Following the occupation of Czechoslovakia, many Czech aircraft were used by the the Luftwaffe as trainers. Seen here on a snow-covered airfield is one of the rarest, a Praga E-241. This was a purpose-built trainer, powered by a Walter 'Pollux' radial engine. The prototype first flew in 1936 and 92 were in service with the Czech training schools at the time of the German occupation. Wearing an all-silver finish, NG+??, is in service with an unknown Luftwaffe training school, probably in winter 1939-40*

29: *Unidentified Luftwaffe flying trainees and a silver Praga E39, construction number 32. This was a Czech designed and built aircraft, several of which found their way into Luftwaffe training service after the annexation of Czechoslovakia. Note the narrow outlined fuselage cross dating from 1939*

30: *Very clear shot of an all-silver Letov (Praga) E-39, a Czech aircraft used extensively for training by the Luftwaffe. Coded ??+GC. The machine is believed to be in service with the Fliegerschule attached to Flieger Ausbildung Regiment 33 based at Elbing in early summer 1940 (AMC)*

31: *Air-to-air picture of an Arado Ar 66, CT+BZ, being flown solo, somewhere in the region of Bad Aibling. Parent unit may be FFS A/B 13 based at Pilsen, Czechoslovakia*

32: *The crew of an Arado Ar 66 of FFS A/B 13 scramble aboard for the next flight from the airfield at Pilsen in Czechoslovakia. The aircraft is unremarkable except for the highly unusual personal marking 'Berta' just above the cross. Apart from one or two other examples seen on other aircraft of this unit (see photo 14) the practice of giving training machines individual markings was practically unknown in the Luftwaffe*

33: *Air to air shot of overall RLM Grau 02 Arado Ar 66 SE+RA, Werk No. 2165, of FFS A/B 8, in flight over Karlsbad. June 1941 (AMC)*

34: *In-flight view of overall RLM grau 02 Gotha Go 145, RP+NR, Werk No 2866, belonging to the flying school (FFS) attached to FAR (Fliegerausbildung Regiment 33) based at Elbing, mid-1940 (AMC)*

35: *Gotha Go 145, RP+NR, Werk Nummer 2866, waits for its pilot. This machine is probably from a flying school attached to FAR 33, based at Elbing in mid-1940*

36: *Go 145, ??+RS, in flight. The unit and location may be FAR 33 in Elbing, 1939*

37: *Arado Ar 65, D-IPOF, apparently newly delivered, sporting a glossy grey, (probably RLM 63) finish with a dark blue fuselage decking and natty coachbuilder's stripe. Date is probably sometime in 1934 (Bruce Robertson)*

38: *An elderly Arado Ar 65 fighter-trainer, coded ?K+OL, serving with FFS A/B 13 at Pilsen in Czechoslovakia taxying out to the runway on a winters day, probably in late 1940. Finish is the typical well-worn RLM 02 Grau with a white spinner*

39: *Port side view of the prototype Arado Ar 68e, D-ITEP, powered by the Jumo 210 engine. The later production Ar 68E briefly equipped the Luftwaffe's fighter squadrons in 1937, but was soon replaced by the superior Messerschmitt Bf 109. Subsequently the Ar 68E saw extensive service with the fighter-training schools (Bruce Robertson)*

40: *WWI fighter ace, Oberstleutnant Theo Osterkamp, wearing only his Pour le Mérite and no other decorations or ribbons in front of a light grey Arado Ar 68E-1, '21', in service as a fighter trainer with JFS 1 at Werneuchen where 'Uncle' Theo was in command until September 1939 when he took over command of JG 51. The underlying fuselage code is the early school marking, S2+??2, indicating Luftkreis 2, which has then had the simpler aircraft number, 21, applied in white over a red band. Date uncertain, but probably 1938-39*

41: *Arado Ar 68E-1, S3+R01, in use as a fighter-trainer, probably somewhere in Luftkreis 3 (HQ in Dresden) as indicated by the barely visible code. Unit and location is most likely FFS A/B 117 at Kamenz in mid-1940*

42: *Flight students of A/B 32 manhandle a ski-equipped overall dark green Arado Ar 68E, DL(?)+VU, onto the start line at Chrudim in Czechoslovakia. This was one of several airfields in the area used by the unit, others were at Pardubice and Sbraslawitz. February 1941. Note the absence of a spinner on the massive wooden propeller*

EAGLES ON THE WING
Training by Combat

The fighter pilots

When World War II began the Luftwaffe possessed a sizeable number of fully trained and efficient aircrew. Despite the loss of such men during the campaigns in Scandinavia, France and the Low Countries, and the even more grievous losses during the Battle of Britain, there was still a sufficient reservoir of crews to sustain operations without major difficulty. Within a year of the ill-judged invasion of Russia, however, this situation quickly changed and the number of trained crews leaving the schools began to be outstripped by the accelerating toll of casualties on the Eastern Front. The most serious shortages were in the ranks of the *Jagdflieger*, where experienced fighter pilots who had survived earlier campaigns were being lost at an alarming rate. Ultimately, the ramifications of the earlier negligence on the part of the Luftwaffe High Command concerning the training of fighter pilots were to be seen in the skies over the Reich itself, where progressively outnumbered German squadrons attempted to deflect the massive Allied aerial armadas.

Until 1942 Luftwaffe commanders had, deliberately or otherwise, been able to ignore the accumulating effects of operational demands upon the training system. By the summer of that year the consequences could no longer be denied and the first units to feel the contraction and deterioration in both the numbers and quality of trained pilots and crews were the fighter squadrons. As previously noted, under the existing system trainees received their basic military training at an FAR, potential NCO pilots and aircrew then passing through the A/B schools, outline details of which were given earlier. Officer candidates, for their part, attended a *Luftkriegschule* for additional training in tactics, air force law, military discipline and regulations etc., as well as the basic flying skills. Brief details of the LK schools, which brought the potential pilot officer up to 'B' Certificate level, can be found in *Table 6*.

Following the award of his pilot's badge, the trainee then joined one of the *Jagdfliegervorschulen* (JVS) for initial fighter training where he was allowed to fly various obsolete or foreign single-seat fighter aircraft. Prominent amongst these were such old-stagers as the Ar 68 and He 51 biplanes, early model Bf 109 and French Dewoitine D.520 monoplanes and assorted captured machines. Initial training was followed by more demanding aircraft and exercises at a *Jagdfliegerschule* (JFS). *Table 7*.

Eventually, the newly fledged *Jagdflieger* was permitted to try out his skills in a fully operational aircraft when he was posted to the IV Gruppe – the *Ergänzungsgruppe*

43 Above: *A Messerschmitt Bf 110C, BO+AW, believed to be in service with an unidentified NJSchule (NJS 1?) or Stuka-Vorschule 1 at Bad Aibling in winter 1940-41 (AMC)*

Table 6

Officer Training Schools – Luftkriegschulen (LKS)

School	Date Formed	Main Bases Used	Comments
LKS 1	January 1940	Dresden, Riesa-Leutewitz, Kamenz	First formed as LKS Dresden, April 1936.
LKS 2	January 1940	Berlin-Gatow, Güterfelde, Reinsdorf	First formed as LKS Berlin-Gatow April 1936. Closed October 1944
LKS 3	January 1940	Wildpark-Werder, Magdeburg, Borkheide, Güterfelde	Formed January 1936 as LKS Werder/Havel. Merged with FFS A 61 at Oschatz May 1944
LKS 4	January 1940	Fürstenfeldbruck, Bad Wörishofen, Neu-Ulm, Kempten-Durach, Schongau	Formed 1937 as LKS Fürstenfeldbruck Closed 1944.
LKS 5	January 1940	Breslau-Schöngarten	Formed March 1939 as LKS Breslau-Schöngarten. Closed September 1944.
LKS 6	Autumn 1944	Kitzingen	Brief existence only.
LKS 7	January 1940	Tulln, Langenlebarn, Budweis, Seyring	Formed October 1939. Existed until December 1944.
LKS 8			Flak unit
LKS 9	1942	Tschenstochau, Werneck	Sport gliding only.
LKS 10	May 1944	Fürstenwalde/Spree	To Straubing January 1945.
LKS 11	End 1944	Straubing	Formed from FFS A/B 121 (qv)
LKS 12	End 1944	Bug am Rügen	Non-flying unit
LKS 13	?	Halle/Saale	Flying only in connection with the signals training unit based there.

Table 7

Jagdfliegvorschulen (JVS)

JVS	Date Formed	Main Bases Used	Comments
JVS 1	?	Kamenz/Saxony	
JVS 2	?	Lachen-Speyerdorf	
JVS 3	?	Vienna-Schwechat, Neubiberg	
JVS 4	?	Fürth	
JVS 5	?	Vienna-Schwechat	

Jagdfliegerschulen (JFS)

JFS	Date Formed	Main Bases Used	Comments
JFS 1	1939	Werneuchen	First formed 1937
JFS 2	1939	Schleissheim	First formed 1934
JFS 3	1939	Stolp-Reitz, Grove, Bad Aibling	
JFS 4	1939	Fürth	
JFS 5	1939	Vienna-Schwechat, Villacoublay, Guyancourt	
JFS 6	?	Lachen-Speyerdorf, Eichborn	
JFS 7	1941	Nancy	Formed from ZVS 1
FFS JGr Drontheim			
FFS JGr Langfuhr			
JG 112	August 1944	Landau/Isar	Fighter conversion school for ex-bomber pilots

44: Starboard view of Arado Ar 76, D-IUSE, in use as a fighter trainer, probably in 1935-36. Note that the fuselage spine is painted, probably in blue. Location uncertain, but possibly Bernburg (AMC)

45: Unusual rear view of an Arado Ar 76 advanced fighter trainer in service with A/B 32, Chrudim, Czechoslovakia, January 1941

46: Arado Ar 76, DH+GF taxies in. Painted overall RLM 02 Grau overall, the aircraft retains the swastika in the early central position on the fin and rudder. Taken from the album of August Diemer, the machine is in service with either LKS 1 or FFS A/B 117, both of which were at Kamenz in 1940-41 when this picture was taken (AMC)

47: *Side view of the first prototype Arado Ar 96, D-IRUU, after it had had the undercarriage, fin, rudder and cockpit canopies modified to early production standard (Bruce Robertson)*

48: *D-IXWZ was the Arado Ar 96 V9, fitted with a rear gunner's position in accordance with a Bulgarian requirement. This was the only aircraft so fitted (Bruce Robertson)*

49: *Trainer Arado Ar 96B, GA+JV, provides off-duty amusement for the ground crews of the US 324th Fighter Group. Despite the battered paintwork, the aircraft is probably in good condition, and the gantry in the background may mean that it has just had an engine change. Werk Nummer 842, is painted in yellow on the fin. Note the glossy finish of the letters compared to the camouflage. Stuttgart-Echterdingen June 1945*

(training group) – of his allotted Geschwader. The intention was to allow the new pilots time to gain precious operational experience before being hurled into the front line. Here, it should be noted, the unit was under the control of the local Luftflotte commander, who was frequently under considerable operational pressure to use whatever forces he had available. As a result the trainee's stay in the IV Gruppe was all too often quite brief.

At first this system worked well enough, but the loss of so many experienced pilots meant that there was insufficient manpower to carry out the training function in the operational squadrons, which therefore became more and more abbreviated. Consequently, the result was the disbandment of the Ergänzungsgruppen attached to specific units in summer of 1942 and the formation of three Fighter Pools situated in the three main operational areas of the Luftwaffe i.e. in the South at Cazaux in France *(ErgänzungsJagdgruppe Süd – EJGr Süd)*; in the West, i.e. of Berlin, based at Mannheim, Germany *(ErgänzungsJagdgruppe West – EJGr West)* and in the East at Krakow in occupied Poland *(ErgänzungsJagdgruppe Ost – EJGr Ost)*. In future, operational units were to draw their replacement crews from these pools. Although this reduced the number of instructors required, however, it also had the effect of curtailing operational training of new pilots at the very time such experience was becoming vitally necessary to the newcomers. Equally seriously, the elimination of what was in effect a fully-crewed, albeit only part-trained reserve in the Ergänzungsgruppen, led to a dilution in front-line strength.

Another aspect of the changed situation was that from spring 1943, the specialised fighter and bomber training schools were put on a more operational footing, ceasing to be designated as fighter schools (JFS), but becoming *Jagdgeschwader* (JG) as shown in *Table 8*.

There were in addition to the above, two *Zerstörerschulen* – Heavy Fighter Schools 1 and 2 – based at Schleißheim and Memmingen respectively and used to train pilots intended for the Messerschmitt Bf 110, Me 410 and Ju 88 fighter squadrons. ZS 2 became ZG 101 in the spring of 1943.

So far, only passing mention has been made of night fighting. The question of intercepting enemy aircraft in the dark had scarcely been considered at the outbreak of war, but as the RAF's nocturnal raids began to become ever more damaging, the Luftwaffe was forced to react. Night fighter pilots were by the nature of their task required to be better trained, most obviously in blind and bad weather flying, than their comrades operating in daylight. With a syllabus that laid heavy emphasis on instrument flying skills, more akin to that of bomber crews, it is perhaps not so surprising to find that there were so few Nachtjagdschulen. The excessive vulnerability of the Zerstörer heavy fighter aircraft by day led to these units converting to night fighting, with an attendant need for training. The first night fighter school was therefore formed at Schleißheim, the pupils receiving their final polish with the training Staffeln of the operational units from 1941 onwards. By the autumn of 1942 other training units had been formed in the south of Germany, their designations reflecting the rather piece-meal nature of the entire night fighter force at that time. Later formations followed the more standardised numbering of semi-operational units begun in spring 1943. *Table 9.*

Table 8

JFS	JG	Main Bases Used
JFS 1	JG 101	Werneuchen, Pau, Schongau
JFS 2	JG 102	Zerbst, Stolp-Reitz
JFS 3	JG 103	Bad Aibling, Chateauroux, Stolp-Reitz, Pütnitz
JFS 4	JG 104	Fürth/Roth
JFS 5	JG 105	Villacoublay, Chartres, Bourges, Guyancourt, Markersdorf
JFS 6	JG 106	Lachen-Speyerdorf, Reichenbach
JFS 7	JG 107	Nancy, Tapolca, Steinamanger, Markersdorf
JFS 8 (A/B 62)	JG 108	Bad Vöslau/Stuhlweissenberg, Wiener-Neustadt
	JG 109	Stolp-Reitz
	JG 110	Altenburg, Graz, Swinemünde
	JG 111	Roth
	JG 112	Landau/Isar

Table 9
Luftwaffe Nightfighter Training Schools

Unit	Date formed	Main Bases Used
NJS 1	1940	Schleißheim
Erg./NJG 1	1942	Stuttgart/Echterdingen
NJS 2	1943?	Stuttgart/Echterdingen
III/NJG 3	1942	Nellingen
8.NJG/3	1942	Ingolstadt
4.NJG/4	1942	Laupheim
NJG 101	1943	Manching, Schleißheim, Munich-Reim
NJG 102	1943	Kitzingen, Powanden, Oels, Prague-Gbell

Many an obsolescent or ex-enemy fighter aircraft found a home in the advanced fighter schools. A few are described in more detail in the following pages.

Arado Ar 68

Last fighter biplane to enter service with the Luftwaffe, the Arado Ar 68 was intended to be a replacement for the Heinkel He 51. A conventional machine with an open cockpit and a neat cantilever undercarriage, the unequal span and chord wings were of wood, covered with ply and fabric. The fuselage structure was typical for the period, being of welded steel tubes covered with metal and fabric, with a distinctively shaped fin and rudder which was to become a hallmark of several later Arado designs. First flown in 1934, the prototype, D-IKIN, powered by a 750 hp BMW VId in-line engine, lacked power. In turn, D-IBAS, the third prototype, was fitted with a new Junkers Jumo 210 liquid-cooled engine which brought performance up to requirements. This version was therefore ordered into production as the Ar 68E. Shortages of the Junkers engines however, led to a decision to begin production of the BMW powered version as the Ar 68F. In late summer 1936, I./JG 134 and I./JG 131 became the first units to be equipped with the type. By the time the Ar 68E started to arrive in the squadrons in spring 1937, the age of the biplane was clearly over. Three Ar 68Es were delivered to Spain for trials as nightfighters, but the far superior Messerschmitt Bf 109 had arrived, consequently most Ar 68 models were quickly transferred to the fighter schools. A few saw service as temporary nightfighters with 10.(N)/JG 53, 10.(N)/JG 72 and 11.(N)/JG 72. Amongst schools known to have used the Ar 68 are A/B 14, A/B 23, A/B 32, A/B 33 and A/B 115. Data for the Ar 68E:

Span:	11.00m / 36 ft 1 in)
Length:	9.50m / 31 ft 2 in)
Weight:	2020 kg / 4454 lb (Fully loaded)
Max Speed:	335 kmh / 208 mph

Heinkel He 51

Developed from a series of little prototype He 49 'sports' biplanes produced during the early 1930's, the Heinkel He 51 was ordered into production before the Luftwaffe officially existed. Ten He 51A-0 aircraft, all civilian registered, were built in 1933, followed by the A-1 series in 1934. These were fully-equipped fighters and formed the first squadron of the resurgent Luftwaffe, JG 132 *Richthofen*, in March 1935. 75 He 51A-1 machines were built, succeeded by a batch of structurally improved B-0 versions. Thirty-eight examples of the B-2 ship-borne floatplane version followed for service on the Kriegsmarine cruisers. An entirely conventional, if rather menacing looking biplane of all-metal construction covered with fabric, powered by a BMW VI in-line engine giving 550 hp and carrying two MG 17 machine guns, the elegant Heinkel was a natural subject for the Nazi propaganda machine. The outbreak of the Spanish Civil War in summer 1936 gave an opportunity to demonstrate the superiority of German aircraft when an initial batch of 6, rapidly followed by another 36, were sent to Spain to aid the Nationalists. All too quickly it became evident that the basic design concept of the He 51 was out-dated. Several aircraft were soon damaged by the type's tendency to bounce and veer on landing. Even worse, the opposing Soviet-supplied I-15 fighters so completely outclassed the Heinkels that they were forced to avoid combat. By April 1937 the He 51 was being relegated to ground attack duties, a role in which, to everyone's surprise, it was extremely successful. The result was the He 51C, fitted with bomb racks for 50 kg bombs intended specifically for low-level close support, 79 of which were built under licence by Fieseler-Flugzeugbau. Under the command of Adolf Galland, the close support He 51 units effectively wrote the manual which was to stand the Luftwaffe in such good stead during World War 2. Overtaken by more modern aircraft, surviving He 51s in Germany were relegated to the fighter schools where their idiosyncratic landing characteristics gave student pilots interesting experiences. Schools known to have used the He 51 include A 43, A/B 71, A/B 120, A/B 123 and LKS 2. Data for the He 51A-1:

Span:	11.00m / 36 ft 1 in)
Length:	8.40m / 27 ft 6 3/4 in)
Weight:	1900 kg / 4189 lb (Fully loaded)
Max Speed:	330 kmh / 205 mph

Dewoitine D 520

The great hope of the French fighter squadrons in 1939, the Dewoitine D 520 was the only fighter in French service at the time of the German assault in May 1940 capable of meeting the Messerschmitt Bf 109E on something like equal terms. Had it not been for the fall of France, it is possible that the D 520 would have enjoyed a similar career to the Spitfire or Bf 109.

A successor to earlier monoplane fighters from the Dewoitine company, the D 520 resulted from a private venture by the company which resulted in an order for two prototypes in April 1938. By October 1938 the first prototype was ready for flight. A low wing all metal monoplane with a retractable undercarriage and an engaging toy-like quality with its long nose and short fuselage, testing quickly discovered a number of shortcomings. D 520-03, the third prototype, incorporated modifications to the tail, cockpit canopy and undercarriage and established the essential features of the production versions. Powered by an Hispano-Suiza 12Y 45 in-line engine of 930 hp,

50: *Focke-Wulf Fw 56 fighter-trainers from JFS 1 at Werneuchen, probably sometime in 1939. The tail and wing in the foreground belong to Arado Ar 68's of the same unit. The quasi-civil WL- letter codes have been overpainted by a series of numbers on coloured bands. Every aircraft on the base would have received an individual number, and it seems that the Fw 56's had a yellow (or possibly white) band with black numbers, while the Ar 68's used a red band with white numbers. This system did not necessarily apply to other units*

51: *Focke-Wulf Fw 56 Stösser, VB+JQ, taxies in after a flight from an unidentified grass airfield. Note the silver finish and the way the Werk Nummer, 2315, on the rudder is divided by the Focke-Wulf company logo. Probably seen here at Pilsen, Czechoslovakia*

52: *Focke-Wulf Fw 56, DB+NN, rather the worse for wear. The rugged construction of the aircraft probably saved the pilot from injury Ð note the unused parachute on the ground (AMC)*

53: *Excellent closeup of student pilot Reum as he climbs aboard Focke-Wulf Fw 56, CA+IB, for a high altitude flight to 4000 m. The overall grey finish shows numerous details, including the yellow fuselage band, the Focke-Wulf company logo just above the strut root, details of the hinged access hatch and the data table below the tailplane. This identifies the machine as belonging to LKS 2 based at Berlin-Gatow, although actual flying took place from Güterfelde and Reinsdorf (AMC)*

54: *Focke-Wulf Fw 56 Stössers on the flight line. Nearest is overall dark green DB+??, which has a yellow fuselage band and lower wing tips. Note the lowered access flap and the student pilot going through his preflight cockpit checks. Next is an overall grey example, CA+??, and further back still another green aircraft, DB+??. DB may have served to identify the unit or may simply have been allocated to a batch of Fw 56 aircraft., the unique last two letters serving to identify the individual machine. The unit is LKS 2 at Güterfelde or Reinsdorf in 1942-43*

55: *Almost a Luftwaffe fighter-trainer, D-EZWA was the prototype Skoda-Kauba V4 which was designed by a team led by Austrian Otto Kauba, based at Cakowitz, near Prague, in 1942. Trials with four improved further prototypes led to the type being ordered into production as a potential standard Luftwaffe trainer aircraft. The whole idea was effectively sabotaged when the first five Czech-built production aircraft were found to be so badly constructed that the whole project was abandoned*

giving a top speed of 332 mph and armed with a 20 mm cannon in the propeller hub and four 7.5 mm machine guns in the wings, the D 520 was a potent weapon. Clearly superior to all other French fighters then in service, 1,280 examples were on order by the outbreak of war. As a result of ill-judged nationalisation, however, the French aircraft industry was in a complete shambles and only 403 had actually been delivered by the time of France's defeat. In fact, only 79 had been accepted by the *Armée de l'Air* by May 10. Those that were delivered acquitted themselves well, being responsible for 108 confirmed air victories between January and June 1940.

With over 320 left on charge, the Germans agreed that production could continue to equip the Armistice Air Force. When the Germans finally occupied the whole of France in November 1942, they seized 245 examples of the D 520 and instructed that another 150 be delivered by June 1944. The Dewoitines were put quickly into service as advanced trainers, a considerable number being passed on to German allies, notably Italy and Bulgaria. Three German fighter training wings were equipped with the little fighter – JG 101 and JG 103 were partially equipped, while JG 105, based at Chartres, was entirely equipped with the type. Few survived the handling of student pilots, only 55 or so remaining to be recaptured by the Allies.

Span: 10.20m / 33 ft 5 1/2 in)
Length: 8.76m / 28 ft 9 in)
Weight: 2783 kg / 6144 lb (Fully loaded)
Max Speed: 535 kmh / 332 mph

Morane-Saulnier MS 230 Et

Flown for the first time in February 1929, the MS 230 was a logical progression in the long line of parasol monoplanes from Morane-Saulnier stretching back to World War 1. Of fabric covered mixed wood and metal construction, with a sturdy wide track undercarriage, the two-seat open cockpit machine quickly proved to be an excellent advanced trainer. Powered by a 230 hp Salmson 9Ab radial engine, about 980 had been delivered to the training units of both the French *Armée de l'Air* and the *Aeronautique Navale* by June 1940. During the course of the type's career, the fin and rudder were enlarged and both wood and metal propellers were used. When France fell, many were captured by the Germans and put to use in the Luftwaffe training units, until an RLM order dated 16 March 1943 ordered that they all be scrapped, along with numerous other foreign types in service with the Luftwaffe.

Span: 10.70m / 35 ft 2 in)
Length: 7.00m / 22 ft 9 in)
Weight: 1,150 kg / 2,533 lb (Fully loaded)
Max Speed: 205 kmh / 127 mph

Training by combat – the bombers

The fortunes of the bomber and transport units had begun to decline in early 1940, when both aircraft and instructional crews from the training schools were requisitioned to take part in the costly air landing operations in Norway and Holland. By doing so, the Luftwaffe staved off the immediate tactical crisis, but stored up problems for the future. This situation was further aggravated by the appalling losses over Crete between April and June 1941 when some 324 transport aircraft were destroyed. By the time of the disaster at Stalingrad in winter 1942-43, where another 500 aircraft and many of their crews were senselessly sacrificed, the training organisation had already been fatally weakened by shortages of fuel and instructors. Some idea of the perpetual difficulties with which the Schools had to cope can be gained by a brief look at the situation in FFS (C) 15 on 21st March 1941:

	Intended	Actual
Instructors	40	26
Auxiliary Instructors	-	8
Flight trainees	160	209
Aircraft	78	48

As described earlier, the prospective Luftwaffe bomber or transport pilot was required to gain his C1 or C2 licence at a *Flugzeugführerschule C* (FFS C) before he was regarded as competent to fly the larger German machines. (Although generally referred to as 'C' licences, strictly speaking they should be known as the ELF-1 and ELF-2 extended pilot licences – *Erweiterter Luftwaffenflugzeug-führerschein*). The demanding syllabus of the C schools meant that appropriately qualified instructors were at a premium, some of the most valuable being ex-Deutsche Lufthansa pilots. These men, who had learnt their trade pioneering long-distance flying in all weathers, were amongst the most experienced pilots in Germany. They were not, however, exempt from the demands of front-line service and the attendant risks. *Table 10.*

As a consequence of the wholesale re-organisation forced upon the Luftwaffe training system in 1943, on 15 October that year most of these schools were re-designated FFS 'B', retaining the same number as before. e.g. FFS (C) 2 became FFS (B) 2. This was an acknowledgement that the Luftwaffe's most pressing need was for fighter pilots and an indication of the rapidly declining strength of the bomber force which was being frittered-away piecemeal. Indeed, by late 1943 the system was almost incapable of producing pilots trained to fly in all weathers.

Table 10

Luftwaffe Advanced Flying Training Schools

School	Date Formed	Main Bases Used	Comments
FFS (C) 1 (Pyritz)	January 1940	Sorau-Niederschlesien Freiwaldau	Formed from Fl-Ausbildungs-stelle Sorau and FWS E Stolp-Reitz. In Sorau until October 1942
FFS (C) 1	February 1943	Schweinfurt, Bayreuth-Bindlach	Converted from A/B 51. As B1 from October 1943 until July 1944
FFS (C) 2	1936	Neuruppin	From Fliegerschule Neuruppin until August 1944
FFS (C) 3	February 1939	Alt-Lönnewitz, Alteno/Nieder-Lausitz, Pretzsch/Elbe, Gahro/Nieder-Lausitz, Prague Letnany?	Became C 3 in January 1940. Until July 1944
FFS (C) 4	November 1939	Sprottau, Aslau/Niederschlesien Sagan-Küpper/Niederschlesien	Until July 1944
FFS (C) 5	April 1934	Neubrandenburg, Anklam	Originally a branch of DVS-Cottbus. C 5 from January 1940 until July 1944
FFS (C) 6	July 1937	Burg b/Magdeburg, Kolberg, Pinnow	To Kolberg October 1939 as FFS (C) Stade. C 6 from January 1940 until July 1944
FFS (C) 7	November 1939	Celle, Finsterwalde, Alteno Clermont-Ferrand, Gablingen	Was FS Celle. April 1943 to Clermont-Ferrand, France. Back to Gablingen April 1944. Possibly became A5 in May. Also at Gardemoen, Norway and Radom, Poland?
FFS (C) 8	January 1940 Đ	Wiener-Neustadt, Eisenstadt, Parndorf, Trausdorf	Was FFS (C) Furth. Closed June 1944
FFS (C) 9	January 1940	Altenburg, Windischenlaibach, Pretzsch/Elbe	Was FFS (C) Kiliansdorf. Part to Mannheim-Sandhofen in May-August 1941 for Ju 88 training. August 1942 all to Pretzsch. Closed September 1944
FFS (C) 10	November 1939	Fürstenwalde/Spree, Neuhardenberg, Eggersdorf	Was FFS (C) Landau. From Erding in January 1940 to F/Spree. Closed June 1944
FFS (C) 11	Summer 1939	Zeltweg/Steiermark	Was FFS (C) Zeltweg. C 11 from January 1940. Closed June 1944
FFS (C) 12	January 1940	Prague/Ruzyne	Until June 1942, then became BFS 3
FFS (C) 13	January 1940	Rosenborn/Zopten, Nancy, Toul, Delme, Roth Kiliansdorf Unterschlauersbach, Öttingen	June 1941 to Nancy, France. February 1942 to Roth Kiliansdorf Closed June 1944
FFS (C) 14	January 1940	Ohlau/Oder	Became C 19 mid-1941
FFS (C) 14 (New formation)	July 1941	Prague/Gbell	Closed July 1944
FFS (C) 15	January 1940	Lüben/Niederschlesien Gablingen, Bourges, Szombathely (Hungary)	September 1940 to Gablingen. January 1943 to France for He 177 training. May 1944 to Hungary, equipment to other schools. Closed October 1944
FFS (C) 16	May 1940	Burg/Magdeburg, Weissenwarthe Sachau/Gardelegen	Closed July 1944
FFS (C) 17	January 1941	Pütnitz, Greifswald	Formed from FFS (See) 2. Closed July 1944
FFS (C) 18	End 1941	Lüben/Niederschlesien, Sch nfeld-Seifersdorf	Closed July 1944
FFS (C) 19	Mid-1941– from C14	Ohlau	Closed June/July 1944
FFS (C) 20	October 1941	Rosenberg/Zopten, Kiev, Rosenborn, Krosno (Poland)	November 1941 to Kiev. To Krosno January 1942. Closed June 1944

Table 10			
\multicolumn{4}{c}{Luftwaffe Advanced Flying Training Schools}
FFS (C) 21	October 1941	Bialystok (Poland), Rosken, Thorn, Hannover-Langenhagen	To Königsberg/Devau November 1943. April 1944 to Thorn, Hannover in June. Closed September-October 1944
FFS (C) 22	October 1941	Wien-Aspern, Oels, Liegnitz	Operational until July 1944
FFS (C) 23	1942	Kaufbeuren	Brief existence only

Eagles in the Clouds

Before he could qualify for the coveted 'C' licence, the trainee needed to learn the methods and techniques of warfare which would make him an effective military pilot. In particular, the demands imposed upon bomber, reconnaissance, transport and naval pilots and crews, who were obliged to fulfil their allotted tasks in all types of weather, led to the early establishment of blind and all-weather flying training schools. The first of these was formed at Celle in 1934 under the cover name *Fliegerschule des DLV, Zweigstelle Celle/Wietzenbrueck*. By September 1939 there were five *Blindflugschulen*, (BFS), as shown in *Table 11*. Significantly, even under the stimulus of all-out war, there were never more than a dozen or so of these schools.

It can be seen that the blind flying schools also fell victim to the upheavals in the training system in October 1943, most of them being renumbered as 'B' schools and contracting the syllabus to B1-B2 level.

Table 11
Luftwaffe Blind Flying Schools

School	Date Formed	Main Bases Used	Comments
BFS 1	October 1935 as Fliegerlehrgang 1	Brandis, Mörtitz/Eilenburg	BFS 1 from January 1940. 15 October 1943 became B 31
BFS 2	November 1938	Neuburg/Donau, Stargard, Brünn	At Stargard from November 1939. BFS 2 from February 1940 and back to Neuburg. May 1942 to Brünn. Became B 32 October 1943. Closed August 1944
BFS 3	December 1939	Königsberg-Devau, Grieslienen, Enzheim, Prague/Ruzyne	June 1941 to Russia, then back to Enzheim. Returned to Grieslienen October 1941. Summer 1942 to Prague. October 1943 became B 33. Closed August 1944
BFS 4	December 1940	Wien/Aspern, Copenhagen-Kastrup	April 1941 to Kastrup. Specialist transport pilots school. October 1943 became B 34. Closed October 1944
BFS 5	December 1939	Rahmel, Marienburg, Stargard, Belgrade, Mielec, Hagenow/Mecklenburg	June 1940 to Stargard. August 1941 to Belgrade for night-fighter crew training. October 1943 became B 35 and moved to Mielec, Poland. December 1943 in Hagenow. Closed August 1944
BFS 6	April 1934 in Celle	Radom, Poland	BFS 6 from 1940. Became BFS 7 in summer 1941.
BFS 6	Reformed June 1941	Wesendorf	Reconnaissance crew school from end 1942. BFS 36 from October 1943. Closed October 1944
BFS 7	December 1939	Insterburg, Radom, Braunschweig-Waggum	From BFS 6, summer 1941. October 1943 became B 37 training ground attack crews. Back to Germany July 1944. Closed November 1944

Table 11
Luftwaffe Blind Flying Schools

School	Date Formed	Main Bases Used	Comments
BFS 8	1941	Belgrade, Stargard, Terespol, Seerappen, Gabbert, Langensalza	From BFS 5. Early 1943 trained heavy transport crews. To Seerappen as B38 October 1943. At Langensalza December 1944
BFS 9	?	Kaunas, Lithuania	Instructors taken for transport service June-September 1943
BFS 10	May 1943 from A/B 33	Altenburg, Pomssen	School for Wilde Sau night-fighter pilots. October 1943 became JG 110 until end of war
BFS 11	July 1943 from A/B 110	Stubendorf, Ludwigslust	Special night ground attack pilot school. Became SG 111 October 1943. Closed end 1944
BFS Schleswig	Mid-1938	Schleswig	Maritime crew selection centre? Disbanded October 1939

56: An highly unusual picture of an Heinkel He 51 fighter-trainer wearing enormous skis. The underwing code appears to be H?+IK, and the oversized swastika just visible on the fin suggests that the date may be winter 1939-40. The location is unknown (AMC)

57: Heinkel He 51, GU+NW, 'white 2' in service with an unidentified training unit. Visible in the background is the tail of an ex-Armée de l'Air North American NA 57 and an Heinkel He 46, ??+NQ. Taken from an album belonging to August Diemer, it is possible that the unit may be FFS A/B 121, based at Straubing, Bavaria, where he qualified as a flying instructor

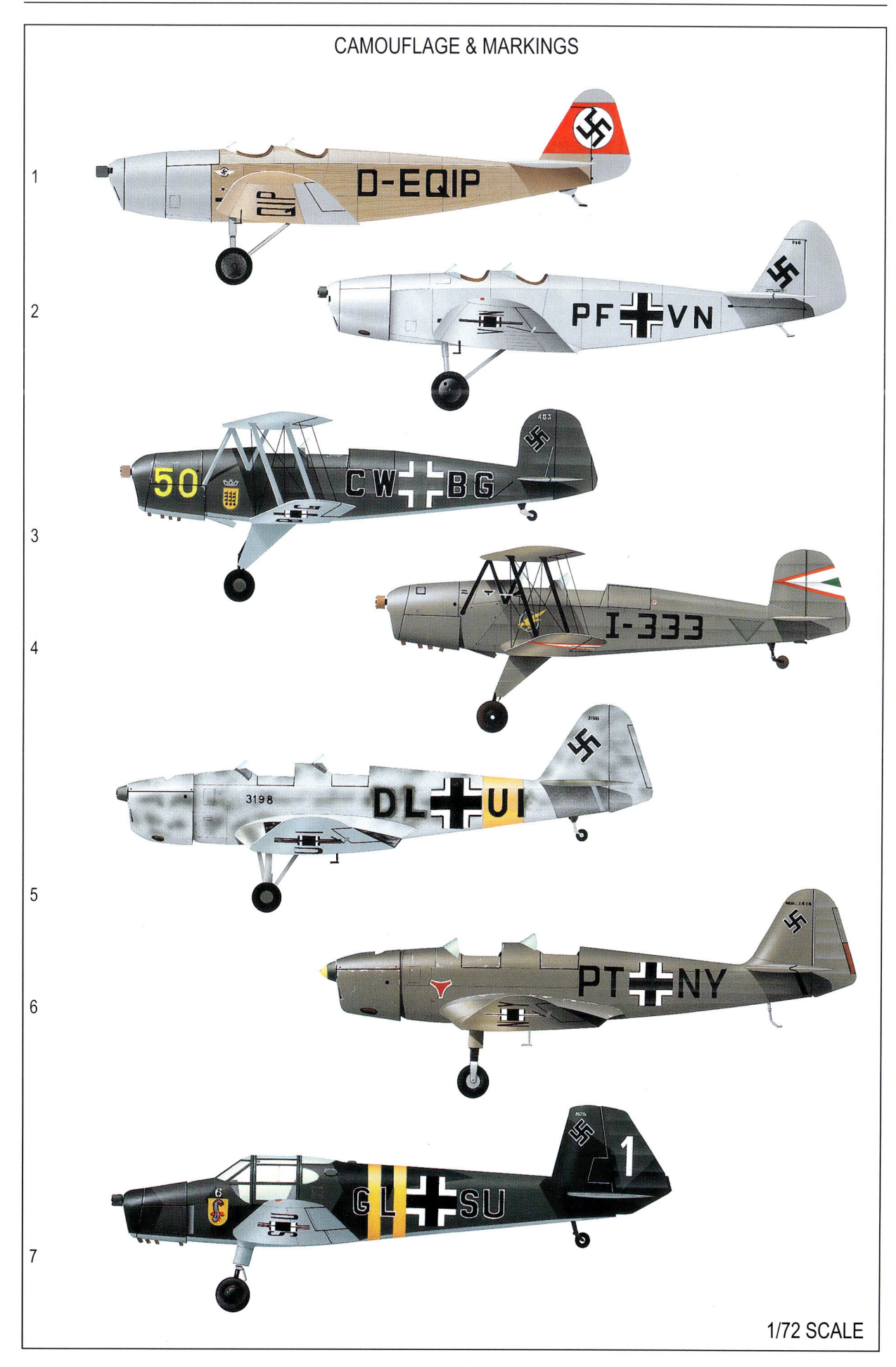

CAMOUFLAGE & MARKINGS

1. D-EQIP
2. PF+VN
3. 50 CW+BG
4. I-333
5. 3198 DL+UI
6. PT+NY
7. GL+SU 1

1/72 SCALE

41

CAMOUFLAGE & MARKINGS

1/72 SCALE

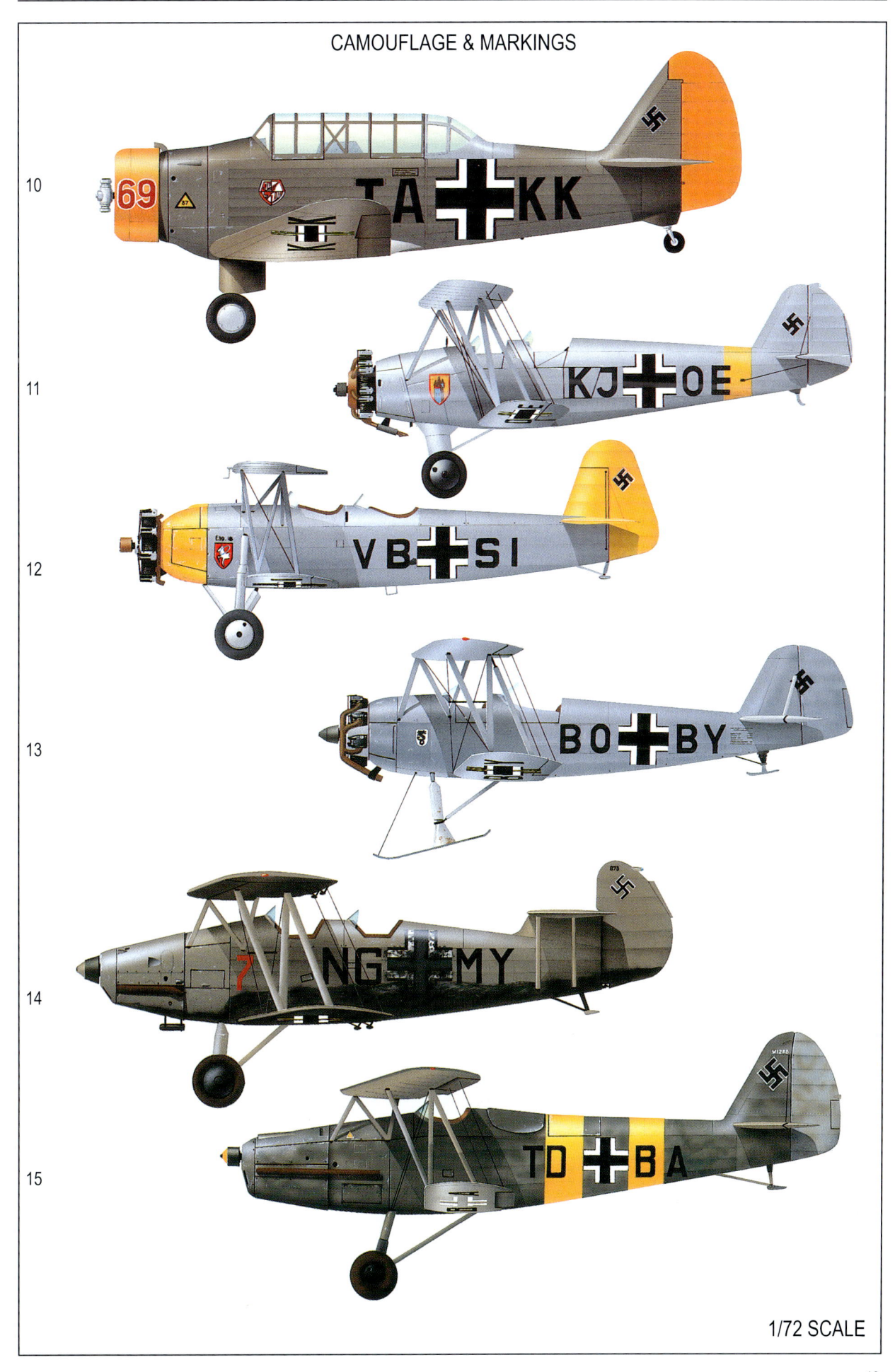

CAMOUFLAGE & MARKINGS

10

11

12

13

14

15

1/72 SCALE

43

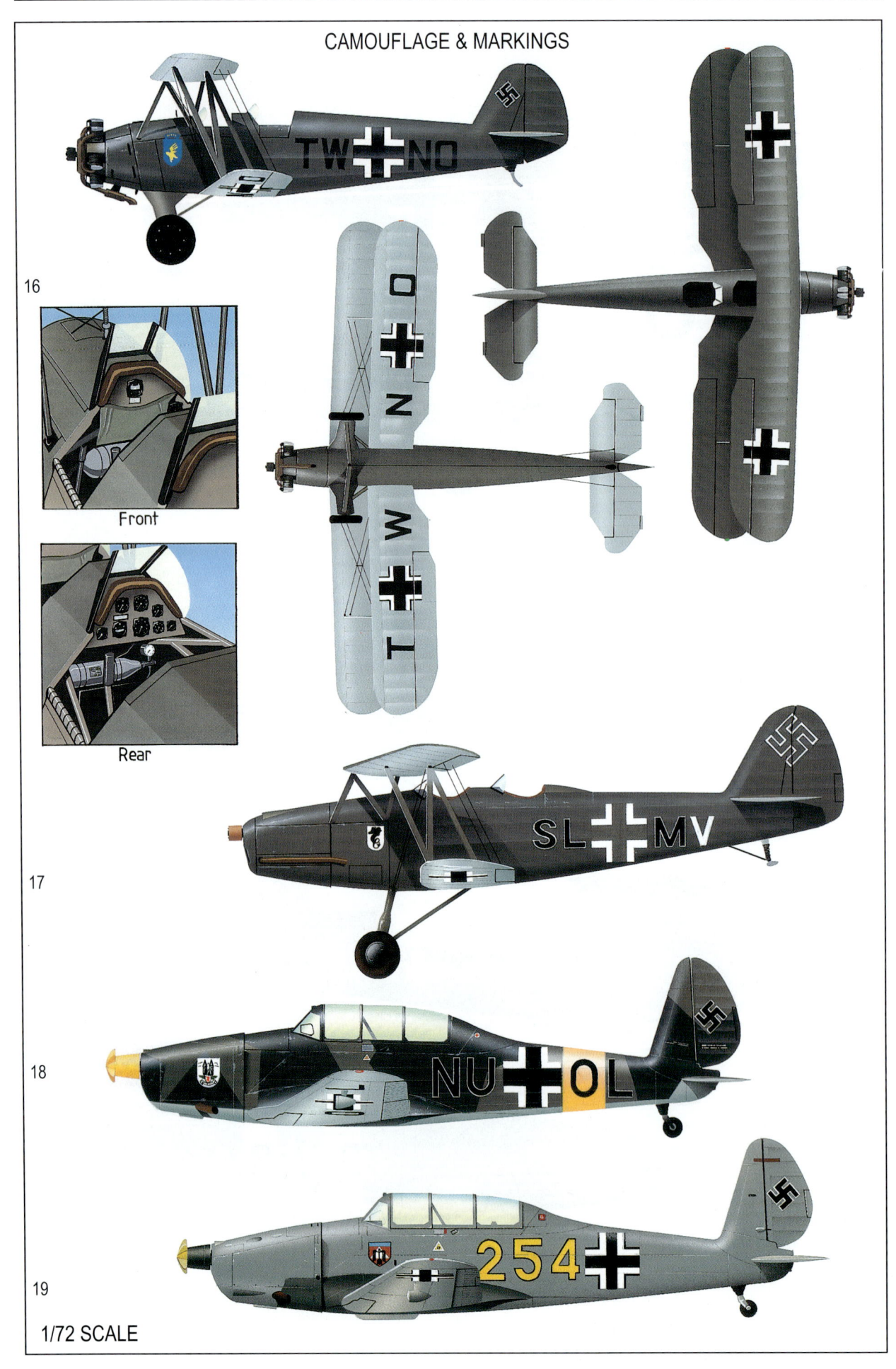

CAMOUFLAGE & MARKINGS

16

Front

Rear

17

18

19

1/72 SCALE

CAMOUFLAGE & MARKINGS

20

21

22

23

24

25

1/72 SCALE

45

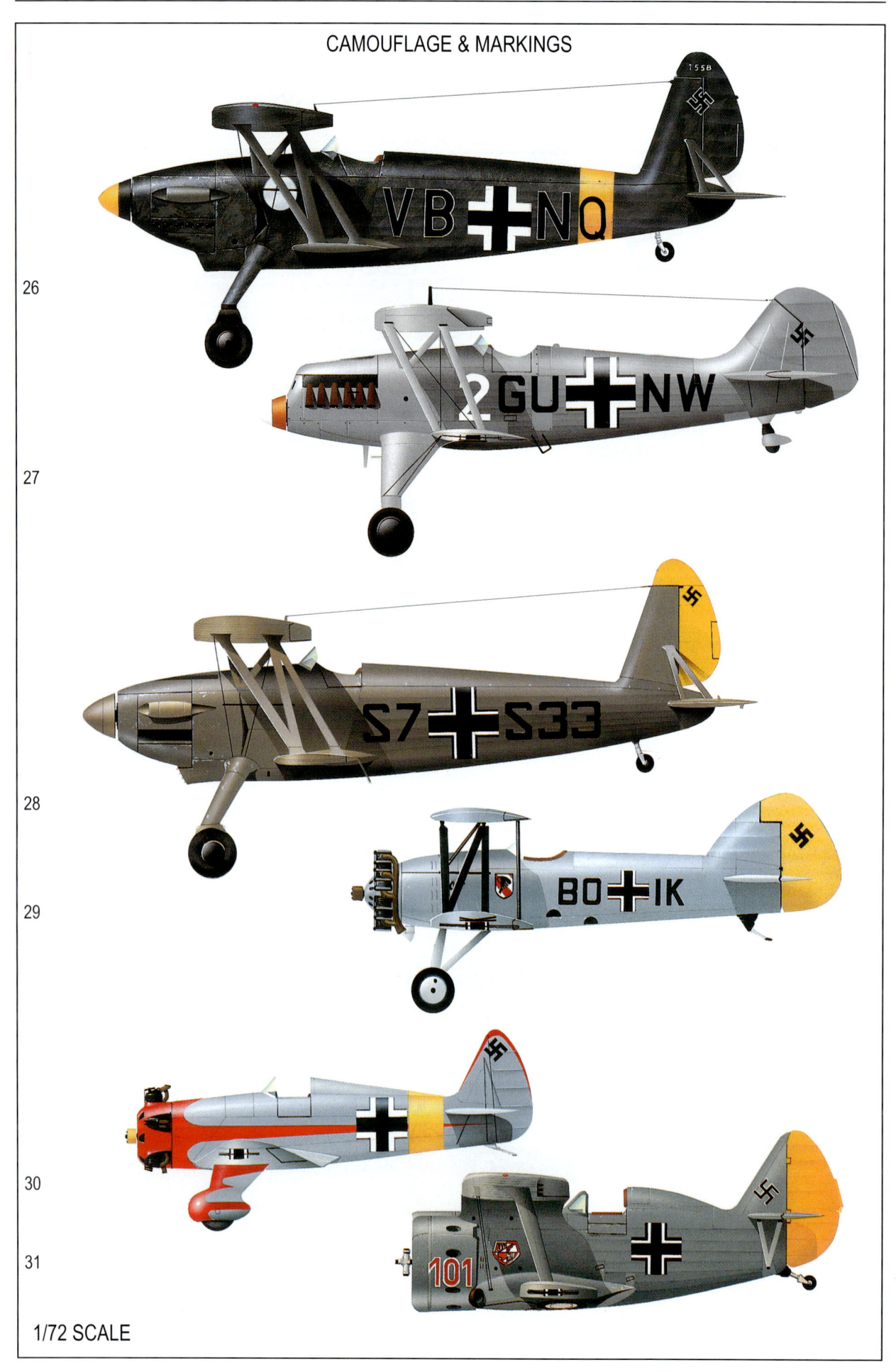

CAMOUFLAGE & MARKINGS

26

27

28

29

30

31

1/72 SCALE

CAMOUFLAGE & MARKINGS

1/72 SCALE

CAMOUFLAGE & MARKINGS

38

39

40

41

42

43

1/72 SCALE

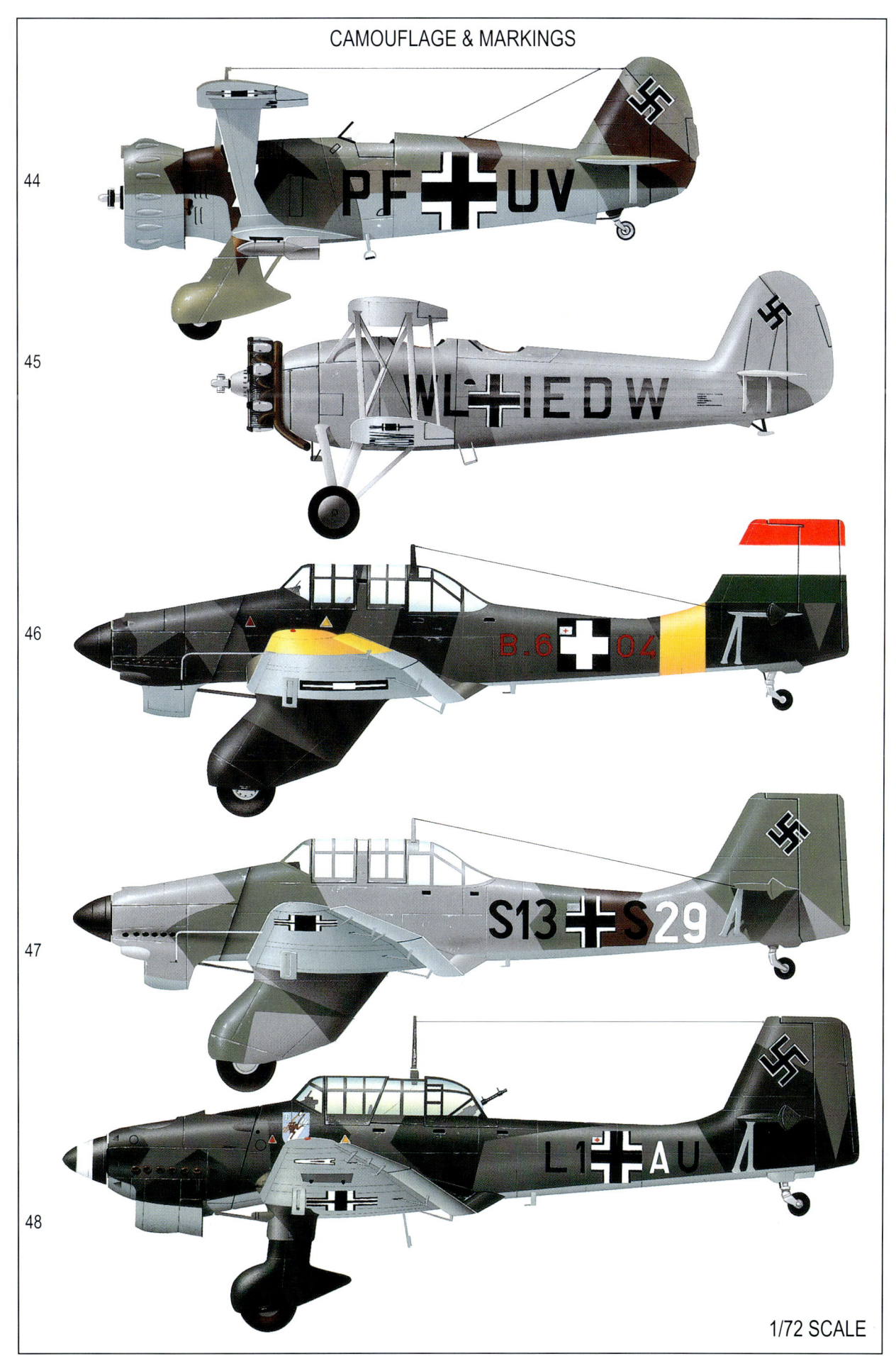

CAMOUFLAGE & MARKINGS

44

45

46

47

48

1/72 SCALE

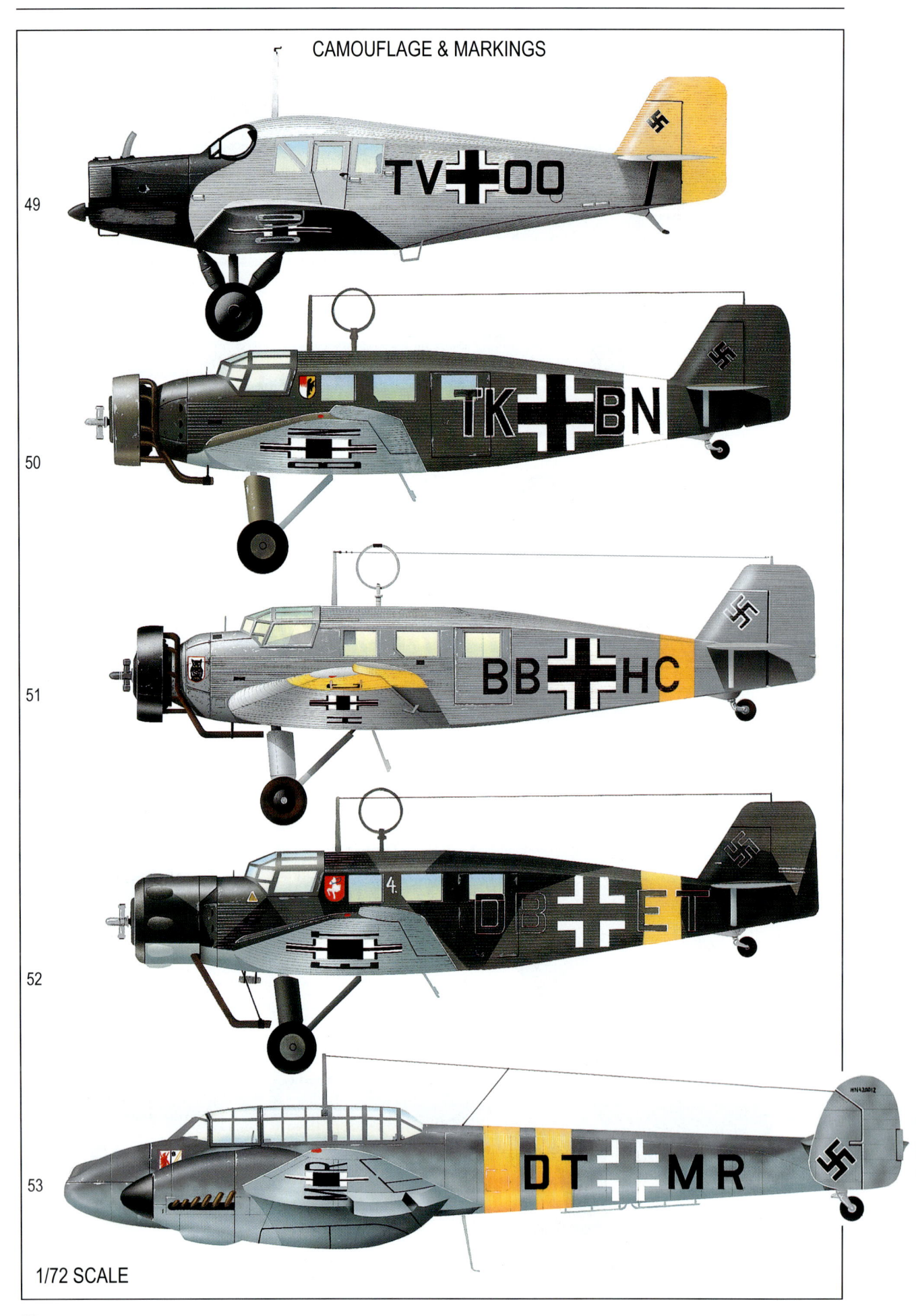

CAMOUFLAGE & MARKINGS

49

50

51

52

53

1/72 SCALE

CAMOUFLAGE & MARKINGS

54

55

56

57

58

1/72 SCALE

CAMOUFLAGE & MARKINGS

59 60 61

1/72 SCALE

CAMOUFLAGE & MARKINGS

62

63

64

1/72 SCALE

CAMOUFLAGE & MARKINGS

1/72 SCALE

65 66 67

CAMOUFLAGE & MARKINGS

68

69

70

71

1/72 SCALE

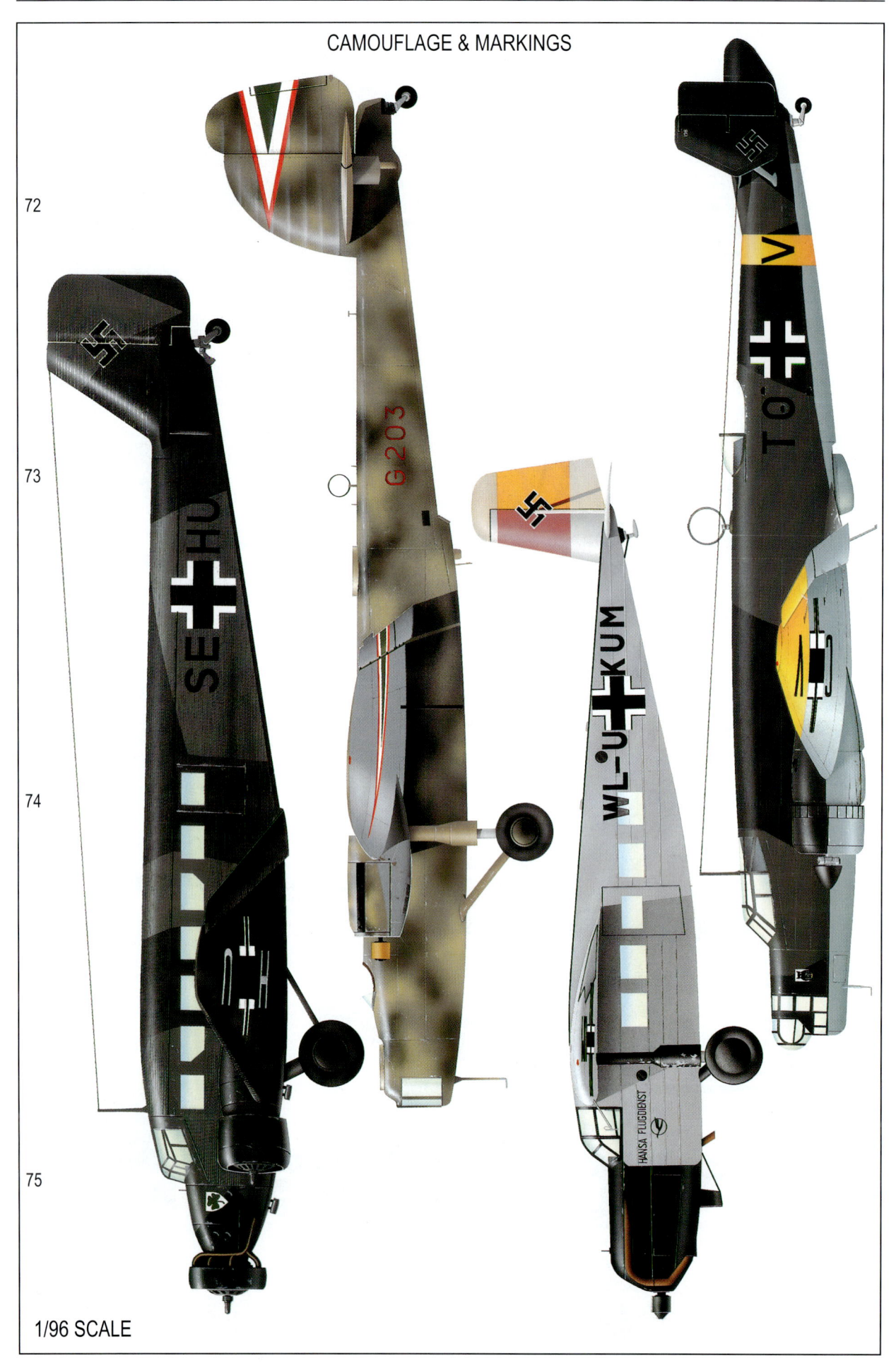

CAMOUFLAGE & MARKINGS

72

73

74

75

1/96 SCALE

58: An old Messerschmitt Bf 109D-1 in use as a fighter trainer with an unknown Luftwaffe training school serves as a backdrop for a picture of the ground crew. The style of the crosses and camouflage scheme, and the huge underwing code letters, PB+??, serve to date the picture to about 1941, probably somewhere in Germany (AMC)

59: Lineup of Messerschmitt Bf 109B fighters in service with JFS 1 as trainers in 1938-39. These machines use a possibly unique variant of the early school identity markings i.e. all the machines carry the 'S2' code which identifies a school in the Luftkreis 2 area, with individual identities of M53, M58 etc. 'M' presumably indicates Messerschmitt. Note how the code on the second machine in line is all black, while the next, M53, has the numbers outlined. By the tones on the photo this outline appears to be yellow

60: Falling standards at the fighter pilot training schools led to a need for an intermediate advanced trainer more closely related to the type of operational aircraft the pilot would eventually fly. The result was a series of two-seat Messerschmitt Bf 109G-12 conversions. CJ+MG was originally a G-6 and served as the prototype for the sub-series (Bruce Robertson)

61: *A derelict Dewoitine D.520, once the pride of the French air force, now abandoned after serving as an advanced trainer with a Luftwaffe fighter school. SN+WS probably served with JG 105 in France (Jerry Scutts)*

62: *All-silver ex-French North American NA 57 serving in a Luftwaffe training school. The aircraft wears narrow 1939-style fuselage crosses, which suggests that it may have been refurbished in France, and was in service with a school in that country*

63: *Czech-built Avia B.534 fighter-trainer, SD+NY, taxying across the field at Pilsen, Czechoslovakia, presumably in use by the instructors of FFS A/B 13*

64: Grey-green finished He 45 with the civilian registration D-ISES. This is believed to be a machine of Aufkl.Gruppe 24, a reconnaissance school which was based at Kassel from 1935, and where the original owner of this picture, Johannes Purnhagen, learnt his trade as an aerial observer (AMC)

65: Port side view of a Heinkel He 45, SP+AB, in training school service. Date, location unknown

66: Dark green Heinkel He 45, coded PF+NT, on a snow-covered Luftwaffe training airfield. The location is possibly one of the cluster of airfields in the Marienbad area in Czechoslovakia, probably winter 1939-40 (AMC)

67: Unknown flight trainees and Heinkel He 46, BO+P?, possibly Werk Nummer 729(?), being readied for flight. Unit and location is believed to be FFS A/B 117, Kamenz 1940 (AMC)

68: Heinkel He 70F, possibly Werk Nummer 1774, wearing the early style of training codes found in the immediate pre-war years. S4+Q22 indicates that the machine belonged to a training school in Luftkreis 4. Unusually, the digits are in white (AMC)

69: An immaculate RLM 02 Grau Heinkel He 50, LP+GY. There is a barely legible Werk Nummer on the fin, possibly 1451. The location is possibly one of the airfields around Marienbad and Karlsbad in Czechoslovakia, probably in winter 1939-40

70 Opposite: Heinkel He 111B-2, NA+EB, of KFS 4, Thorn (Torun) in occupied Poland running up its engines ready for takeoff. The aircraft here clearly shows the elliptical wing shape used on the early versions of the He 111 which was inherited from its predecessor, the Heinkel He 70 (AMC)

EAGLES ON THE WING
Sharpening the talons

In the same way that a fighter pilot had to be more than an aerial chauffeur in order to be militarily effective, so the prospective bomber pilot or crew member needed to learn the military tactics and skills appropriate to his calling. The last stage of training before a pilot was posted to an operational unit was a spell at a weapons school (or at least this was the intention until the re-organisation of training in 1943). Having a similar function to an RAF OTU (Operational Training Unit), the first three of these *Grosse Kampffliegerschulen* – Bomber Schools – were already in existence in September 1939, KFS 4 being re-formed in early 1940 in newly occupied Poland. Also known as *Waffen Schulen* – Weapons Schools – it should be noted that in line with the German system of training entire crews, these units also trained observers, radio operators and air gunners. *Table 12.*

The first ominous signs in the breakdown of bomber crew training began at the same time as the fighter training programme was being re-organised. Initially, a temporary shortage of aviation fuel led to restrictions in the number of flying hours in bomber training. Shortly afterwards, the catastrophe at Stalingrad proved to be a turning point for the bomber force, when the loss of so many instructor pilots and aircraft led first of all to a severe hiatus in the flow of pupils through the bomber schools and then to an enforced re-structuring of the whole training programme.†

As an emergency measure, bomber pilots were no

Table 12	
Unit	Main Bases Used
KFS 1	Tutow
KFS 2	Fassberg, Hörsching-Linz
KFS 3	Lechfeld, Warsaw-Okecie, Barth, Greifswald (Originally formed in 1935 as an aerial gunnery school)
KFS 4	Thorn (Torun)
KFS 5	Parow, near Stralsund*

*Parow was also home to a weapons school, *Fliegerwaffenschule (See) 3, Dievenow,* used by maritime air units)

† *One of the many possible reasons for the Luftwaffe High Command under-estimating the need for transport aircraft with such dramatic effects upon the training system was the existence of Deutsche Lufthansa. The German state airline had had Erhard Milch, Göring's deputy, as a member of the Board since 1926. Due in part to his influence the airline was regarded as a ready-made military transport arm – indeed on the outbreak of war 22 aircraft and crews were promptly requisitioned. The easy availability of this organisation, however, may have blinded the Luftwaffe Staff to the need for proper planning, as DLH had only 145 aircraft in total in September 1939 – an hopelessly inadequate number to support military operations when it is realised that over 300 aircraft were lost on Crete alone.*

longer to be trained on multi-engined aircraft at schools, but were to learn their trade, on the job as it were, by flying as second pilots on Junkers Ju 52/3m transport aircraft. Apart from the immediate loss in efficiency of the transport squadrons, the disruption caused a surplus of partly trained pupils in the A/B schools, and a shortage of fully trained crews ready to move from the advanced training schools into the reserve squadrons. In a move typical of the piecemeal fashion in which training was approached in the Luftwaffe, the specialist bomber schools were therefore disbanded and their function dropped onto the reserve training units of the operational bomber Geschwader. This was the exactly opposite approach to the fighter squadrons, and was doomed to failure for precisely the same reasons that the method had had to be abandoned by their fighter comrades, i.e. they had insufficient numbers of trained instructor pilots and aircraft. The result of this was that the partly trained pupils were sent directly to the operational units themselves, whereupon the effectiveness of the squadrons was immediately compromised, losses in men and machines escalated and the offensive power of the bomber force was rendered largely impotent.

In the early part of the war, the land-based C schools were endowed with quantities of obsolete or war-weary front line aircraft, mostly of the types listed as follows, but also with a few of the B2 types:

C2 Land: Do 11, Do 23, Do 17, He 111, Ju 52/3m,
   Ju 86, Ju 88, Si 204.

As the war progressed, a trickle of more advanced aircraft, such as the He 177 bomber, found their way to the schools. Shortages of suitable aircraft meant that captured foreign machines were equally acceptable, in particular the French Caudron C.445 and similar types saw extensive service as navigation and instrument trainers before crews commenced instruction on the heaviest C types proper. Brief details of some of the less well known of these types follow:

Dornier Do 23

First flown in 1934, the ponderous Dornier Do 23 bomber was a development of the earlier Do 11 and Do 13 incorporating modifications intended to strengthen the airframe and reduce vibration. The first version, known as the Do 23F was quickly followed by the main service type, the Do 23G. Powered by two BMW VId in-line engines of 750 hp each, the machine was intended to be a supplement to the main Luftwaffe bomber then in service, the Junkers Ju 52/3m. Already obsolescent in engineering terms, the tubular steel structure, mostly fabric covered, was always structurally suspect. The type also left much to be desired in terms of handling and speed, the massive fixed and spatted undercarriage not helping in this respect. Freed from the necessity to disguise their true purpose after the Luftwaffe was revealed to the world, later types of aircraft offered far superior performance and the 200 or so Do 23's built were quickly passed on to the advanced training schools.

Span:	25.60m / 84 ft 0 in)
Length:	18.80m / 61 ft 8 in)
Weight:	9200 kg / 20,290 lb (Fully loaded)
Max Speed:	262 kmh / 163 mph

Junkers Ju 86

The first Junkers design to move away from the corrugated structure which had been a trademark of the company since 1919, the Junkers Ju 86 was designed in response to a joint military and civil requirement for a twin-engined aircraft suitable for use as an airliner or bomber. Retaining a family relationship with earlier Junkers types in the shape of the wing and the double-wing flaps, the twin-tail low wing monoplane made use of a narrow track retractable undercarriage which which was to be a source of problems throughout its service. The intended powerplants of innovative Junkers Jumo diesel engines of 600 hp each were not available for the first prototype, consequently these were fitted to the Ju 86V3, D-ALAL, which first flew in April 1935 in military configuration. A pre-production batch of thirteen followed in early 1936. At the same time work was proceeding on the civilian version, for which the V2, D-ABUK was the prototype. Following various modifications, KG 152 *'Hindenburg'* received the first production Ju 86A-1examples in spring 1936, just as the first 10-seat Ju 86B airliners reached Lufthansa. By the end of the year both bomber and civil versions had been exported to a number of countries, in every case powered by conventional air-cooled piston engines. Problems with stability led to the introduction of the military Ju 86D with an extended tail-cone and greater fuel tankage. The greatest problem, however, was the chronic unreliablity of the diesel engines, consequently BMW-built versions of the Pratt & Whitney Hornet radial engine were fitted to the Ju 86E. This model began to replace the Ju 86D in squadron service from late summer 1937. Further developments were a batch of 40 or so Ju 86G models with redesigned front fuselages intended to give better pilot vision. By the autumn of 1938, experience in the Spainish Civil War had led to the conclusion that the Ju 86 in any current version was not a good bomber – the rather erratic flight characteristics making accurate bomb aiming very difficult.

With the arrival of the greatly superior He 111 and Do 17 bombers into service, the decision was taken to withdraw the 235 examples of the Ju 86 in its several versions from front line use and transfer them to secondary duties. Development of the basic airframe into the long

71: *Focke-Wulf Fw 58C, DK+FF, wears an unusual camouflage scheme of RLM 02 grey overall with dark green, probably RLM 71, over the spine of the fuselage, the nose and on wing uppersurfaces. Believed to belong to FFS A/B 8, then at Vilseck, in 1940/41, the aircraft could be in service with LKS 7, which operated a very similar machine coded DK+FE*

72: *Pilot's view of the instrument panel of a Focke-Wulf Fw 58*

73: *Focke-Wulf Fw 58B, KY+NF, undergoing maintenance. The odd squiggles just behind the nose glazing are red primer paint after small repairs. Overall colour of this machine is RLM Grau 02, a greenish-grey colour. KFS 4 Thorn (Torun) Poland, 1940 (AMC)*

74: What the trainee bomb-aimer saw. View through the nose glazing of a Focke-Wulf Fw 58B showing the Ikaria rotating gun mount also fitted to the Heinkel He 111

75: Focke-Wulf Fw 58C, NV+KX, finished overall RLM 02, with a yellow fuselage band and carrying the elegant winged griffon badge of FFS A/B 71, probably flying out from Proßnitz (R.L. Ward)

76: More than twenty years after the prototype first flew, odd examples of the venerable Junkers F13, ancestor of the Ju 52/3m, were still to be found in service with the Luftwaffe training schools. A few even found employment in the night harassing role on the Eastern Front armed with light bombs and machine guns. Werk Nummer 621, seen here, coded TA+?? is probably in service with an unidentified training school. Its exact ancestry remains uncertain as it seems never to have appeared on the German civil register. Note the yellow tail (R.L. Ward)

wingspan, high altitude Ju 86P and R reconnaissance versions continued well into the mid-war years. Small numbers of these were converted from existing Ju 86D airframes, but the bulk of the remainder went to the bomber schools where they provoked a classic example of the in-fighting amongst the Luftwaffe commanders which bedevilled it until the final collapse.

Faced with growing demands for transport aircraft in early 1940, the front commanders were already requisitioning the Junkers Ju 52/3m transport aircraft, and their instructor crews, which had become the standard training machine in the C schools. This had been logical when no alternative aircraft existed, but no other aircraft in service used three engines and a steering wheel. However, it seemed sensible to the Chief of Staff of the training arm, *Generalmajor* Hans Deichmann, that the Ju 52 be turned over to the transport squadrons and the Ju 86 substituted in the training units. The Ju 86 was not wanted by any other part of the Luftwaffe and, in 1940, the manufacturers still had components for another 1000 examples. With new petrol engines and dual controls the Ju 86 could have become a useful, though short-ranged training machine, when the civilian legacy of its roomy fuselage made it an ideal flying classroom. This eminently practical suggestion was rejected by Erhard Milch, Göring's deputy, on the grounds that all production capacity was needed for the Ju 88. This reasoning is suspect as Milch himself was far from convinced of the potential of the Junkers 'Wonder Bomber'. Possibly he wished to reduce the stranglehold Junkers was developing upon the German aircraft industry (in 1938 Junkers employed 53% of the entire German aviation industry's workforce). Whatever the reason, a logical solution to a growing problem was ignored, the training units were condemned to act as a reservoir of transport crews and aircraft and the training system was doomed to slow decline – but logic was never a strong feature of the Nazi hierarchy. Those models of the Ju 86 which did reach the schools, amongst them the radio school at Halle/Saale, LKS 13, gave sterling service until finally worn out. Data for the Ju 86D-1:

Span:	22.50m / 73 ft 9 3/4 in)
Length:	17.60m / 57 ft 9 in)
Weight:	8200 kg / 18080 lb (Fully loaded)
Max Speed:	300 kmh / 186 mph

Siebel Si 204

A considerably enlarged development of the neat little Siebel Fh 104, the Siebel Si 204 was developed during 1940-41 by a team led by Dipl. Ing. Fecher from Siebel Flugzeugwerke of Halle as a light transport, liaison aircraft and crew trainer. An all-metal low wing monoplane with a dihedral tail with twin fins and rudders, the twin-engined machine could carry up to eight passengers and two crew. The Si 204V1 first flew in May 1941, powered by two 360 hp Argus As 411 in-line engines driving two-bladed propellers and had a stepped windscreen similar to the Fh 104. Series production of the Si 204A started shortly afterwards. A year later the more powerful Si 204D appeared, fitted with a bulbous glazed nose not unlike the Ju 188. Succeeding the Fw 58 into service as the standard Luftwaffe crew trainer, Si 204 aircraft were produced by SNCAC in France, who turned out about 150 between 1942 and the liberation, and Aero in Czechoslovakia. Most of the Si 204D models were produced in Czechoslovakia, approximately 1,007 being delivered between June 1942 and the end of 1944. Although most machines served as radio, radar or navigation trainers, armed versions were developed for use as light bombers, while a few even saw service as radar-equipped nightfighters. The V22 and V23 served as prototypes for the Si 204E fitted with a revolving glazed gun turret in the dorsal position mounting a single MG 131 machine gun and an internal bomb bay capable of carrying up to 500 kg of light bombs. Post-war, the agreeable flying characteristics and robust structure of the type led to development and production continuing in both France, as the NC Martinet, and Czechoslovakia as the C-103/C-3. Luftwaffe training units known to have used the Si 204D include FFS (B) 11 and FFS (C)14. Data for Si 204D follows:

Span:	21.33m / 39 ft 6 in)
Length:	11.95m / 39 ft 2 1/2 in)
Weight:	5,600 kg / 12,350 lb (Fully loaded)
Max Speed:	364 kmh / 226 mph

Ground Attack Schools

In keeping with their specialist roles, there were other types of flying training schools, notably the *Stuka Vorschulen* and *Stuka Schulen* for potential dive-bomber crews. Brief details of the type of training given there were described earlier. However, the changing nature of air warfare meant that the technique of precision dive-bombing of ground and naval targets gradually began to give way to less hazardous methods. Subsequently, the conversion of the operational dive-bomber units from the venerable Ju 87 onto the totally different Hs 129 and ground-attack versions of the Fw 190 eventually led in October 1943 to the wholesale re-designation of the dive-bombing units of the Luftwaffe from *Stuka* to *Schlacht* – literally 'Battle' i.e. ground attack. The new equipment demanded a very different training syllabus and the Stuka schools were accordingly modified and renamed *Schulschlachtgeschwader*. These units, in line with later Luftwaffe training policy, were semi-operational and their designations reflected this. Favourite aircraft of the initial training units were the Hs 123 and He 50 biplanes and early models of the Ju 87. *Table 13.*

Table 13
Luftwaffe Ground Attack Schools

Unit	Date Formed	Main Bases Used	Comments
Stuka Vorschule 1	1940	Bad Aibling	
Stuka Vorschule 2	1939	Graz	
Stuka Vorschule 3	1941	San Damiano (Italy)	
Stuka Schule 1	1939	Kitzingen, Wertheim	
Stuka Schule 2	1939?	Graz-Thalerhof, Piacena (Italy)	
St.G 101	1942	Wertheim	SS 1 renumbered December 1942.
St.G 102	1942	Graz-Thalerhof, Foggia (Italy)	
St.G 103	194?	Metz	
St.G 151	1943	Agram	Formed from the IV Gruppen of the operational units in May 1943.

Schulschlachtgeschwader

Unit	Date Formed	Main Bases Used	Comments
SG 101	1943	Reims, Wischau, Aalborg-West, Paris-Orly, Brünn	St.G 101 renumbered October 1943. Closed December 1944.
SG 102	1943	Paris-Orly, Agram, Deutsches-Brod	
SG 103	1943	Metz, Lyons, Fassberg	
SG 104	1943	Tutow, Aalborg-West	
SG 108	1943		ex JG 108
SG 111	1943	Stubendorf/OS, Ludwiglust	ex BFS 11 from December 1943.
SG 151	1943	Agram, Grove	Renumbered from St.G 151 October 1943.
SG 152	1943	Deblin-Irena (Poland)	Combined with SG 151 in August 1944.

Eyes for the Eagles

Associated with the 'C' schools were the various specialist schools where the requisite skills necessary for other crew members were taught. Among these were the vitally important training schools for reconnaissance pilots and observers – the *Aufklärerschulen*. The operational units which these schools served were divided into two broad types based on their primary functions, namely *Nahaufklärer* – tactical or close reconnaissance in support of operations by the army in the field (known as Army Co-operation in the RAF), and long-range *Fernaufklärer* carrying out strategic missions in support of operational planning. The future reconnaissance crews were selected and trained as such. For the first time they were exposed to aircraft fully equipped with an abundance of special equipment including automatic and hand-held cameras, drift-sights, etc. In addition, the special flying techniques so necessary in aerial photography were taught here. *Table 14*.

Main aircraft equipment of these schools was a selection of He 45, He 46, He 70 and Hs 126 single-engined aircraft and Do 17, Bf 110, Ju 86 and Ju 88 twin-engined machines. Oddly, one of the mainstays of the short-range reconnaissance squadrons, the Fw 189, does not seem to have seen much service with the training schools. Later in the war far more potent aircraft, such as camera-equipped versions of the Bf 109, Fw 190 and the jet-powered Me 262 and Ar 234 were necessary to stand any chance of accomplishing missions.

Table 14
Luftwaffe Reconnaissance Schools

Unit	Date Formed	Main Bases Used	Comments
Aufklärerschule 1	1939	Grossenhain/Saxony	Became I.(F)/101 in early 1943. Closed 1944.
Aufklärerschule 2	1939	Brieg	Became I.(H)/102 early 1943.
Aufklärerschule 3	1939	Jüterbog	Became II.(H)/102 in early 1943
Fliegerbildschule Hildesheim			Formed at Hildesheim in 1935 for training, testing of cameras and photo-interpretation. Active until late in the war.

Heinkel He 45

Originally conceived as a general purpose light bomber in response to a requirement of the clandestine Luftwaffe in 1930, the cumbersome He 45 was a typical Heinkel product of the time; a rugged, but unimaginative two-seat biplane design, powered by a single 750 hp BMW VI liquid-cooled engine driving a massive two bladed wooden propeller. The fuselage was of welded tubular steel with metal panels covering the upper fuselage decking and engine, while the remainder and the all-wooden wings were fabric covered. Three prototypes flew in spring 1932; the He 45a, He 45b and He 45c. A production order for 418 unarmed He 45A and 90 He 45B models equipped with one fixed forward-firing MG 17 and one MG 15 on a ring mounting for the observer followed in the autumn, shortly before Adolf Hitler became Chancellor of Germany. Most aircraft were built by Focke-Wulf and BFW owing to lack of space at Heinkel's Warnemünde factory.

By 1934, with better bomber aircraft available, the He 45 was issued instead to the reconnaissance units where they gave adequate if uninspired service. Numerically, they were probably the most important aircraft in the Luftwaffe inventory at the time.

Experience in Spain during the Civil War ensured that by the outbreak of World War 2 all but 21 of the surviving aircraft of the type were in training units, where their rugged construction was of considerable value. FFS A/B 24 is just one training school known to have used the He 45.

Span:	11.50m / 37 ft 8 3/4 in)
Length:	10.00m / 32 ft 9 3/4 in)
Weight:	2745 kg / 6053 lb (Fully loaded)
Max Speed:	290 kmh / 180 mph

Heinkel He 46

Another of the first generation of aircraft for the newly-emergent Luftwaffe, the He 46 was unusual in that the prototype He 46a was a biplane, while the production versions were parasol monoplanes! Built in 1931 in response to an RWM requirement for a two-seat open cockpit tactical reconnaissance and army cooperation aircraft, early trials proved both that the machine was underpowered and the lower wing seriously impaired the observer's view. Consequently, the third of three prototypes was built as a monoplane with strut braced wings, powered by a 660 hp Bramo 322B radial engine and armed with a moveable MG 15 machine for defensive purposes by the observer. Following conventional Heinkel practice, the mixed steel and wooden structure was covered mostly in fabric.

After official acceptance, production of the first 371 He 46C-1s began at Warnemünde in 1933. This version could carry either a camera or up to 200 kg of small bombs in an underfuselage bay. The pressures upon Heinkel were such that sub-contractors such as Fieseler and Gotha were needed to ensure that deliveries began in early 1935. Six D series aircraft, differing only marginally from the C-1 were built, followed by the E model which differed most obviously from other series by being fitted with a cowling for the radial engine. Problems with the engines meant that these cowlings were usually removed in Luftwaffe service, although fourteen unarmed He 46F-1 and F-2 models for training, powered by 560 hp Armstrong Siddeley Panther engines, retained theirs.

By 1936 the Nahaufklärerstaffeln were completely equipped with the He 46, some of the last examples produced going to Bulgaria (18 C-2s) and Hungary (36 E-2Un). About thirty were sent for trials in Spain, where they suffered heavy casualties in the Civil War. From the spring of 1938, the He 46 began to be replaced by the Henschel Hs 126 and by September 1939 only a few survived in front-line Luftwaffe service. Most of the remaining machines were sent to the training schools, the graveyard of many a Luftwaffe aeroplane, although in 1943 a number were pressed into service for night harassing operations with the Nachtschlachtgruppen on the Eastern Front. Data for He 46C:

Span:	14.00m / 45 ft 11 in)
Length:	9.50m / 31 ft 2 in)
Weight:	2300 kg / 5071 lb (Fully loaded)
Max Speed:	250 kmh / 155 mph

Other Units

So far little has been said of the other essential members of the multi-engined aircraft crews in the Luftwaffe. As indicated earlier, there were specialist schools for training navigators *(beobachter)*, radio operators *(bordfunker)* and flight engineers *(bordmechaniker)*, but apart from a list of *Luftflottennachrichtenschulen* (Air Fleet Signals Schools) most of these seem to have gone undocumented. *Table 15:*

Briefly, the time needed to train a navigator was some six months, that for a radio operator being a year. Eventually the individual members were assembled at the Waffenschulen as a complete crew, where they carried out plotted flights, by day and night, formation flying and bombing exercises. They were then posted together to their operational unit.

The radio and navigation schools in particular made extensive use of the ubiquitous Junkers W 34, Focke-Wulf Fw 58, and later the Siebel Si 204, all with roomy fuselages

Table 15	
Unit	Main Bases
Luftflottennachrichtenschule 1	Nordhausen
Luftflottennachrichtenschule 2	Königgrätz
Luftflottennachrichtenschule 3	Pocking, Gablenz, München-Reim
Luftflottennachrichtenschule 4	Budweis, Deutsch-Brod, Lyons
Luftflottennachrichtenschule 5	Erfurt
Luftflottennachrichtenschule 6	Dievenow

and docile handling which made ideal flying classrooms:

Focke-Wulf Fw 58 *Weihe* (Kite)

One of the true workhorses of the Luftwaffe, Kurt Tank's Fw 58 was the German equivalent to the Avro Anson. First flown as a six-seater civil transport in 1935, it rapidly developed into numerous military versions ranging from crew trainer to ambulance and even crop sprayer.

Apart from being the first Focke-Wulf aircraft to have a retractable undercarriage, the prototype, D-ABEM, which first flew in summer 1935, was an entirely conventional low wing monoplane. Built from steel tubing with a combination of wood, metal and fabric covering and powered by two 240 hp Argus As 10C air-cooled engines. The very sturdy wing centre section was braced to the fuselage by single struts and an important feature was the ability to change the nose section for different roles. In the passenger V1 this was smoothly streamlined, while on the V2 military prototype provision was made for an open gun position. Only a few of the Fw 58A, production version of the V2, were built before interest moved to the Fw 58B. This was one of the main military versions and featured a glazed nose with a bubble mounting for an MG 15 machine gun and the ability to carry bombs. Some were completed as floatplanes, known as the Fw 58BW.

Main production centred on the Fw 58C, a light transport with a solid nose and accommodation for six passengers. D-ALEX, one of the first of these, became Kurt Tank's personal aircraft, in which he was later unsuccessfully attacked by two Spitfires.

Known affectionately as the *Leukoplastbomber* – elastoplast bomber – by German pilots, the Fw 58 saw considerable use in the training schools, as a light transport for the staff of operational squadrons and, not least, casualty evacuation. About 30 were specially modified to allow spraying of areas on the Eastern Front where there was a risk of disease to German troops. One of these, *Werk Nummer* 2093, coded TE+BK, once in service with Ekdo 40, was captured at Fassberg at the end of the war and was sent to England for study of its spraying equipment by the RAE at Farnborough.

The *Weihe* was also exported to Argentina, Bulgaria, China, Holland, Hungary, Romania and Sweden. Twenty-five were built under licence in Brazil. Data for the Fw 58C:

Span:	21.00m / 68 ft 10 3/4 in)
Length:	14.00m / 45 ft 11 1/4 in)
Weight:	3600 kg / 7936 lb (Fully loaded)
Max Speed:	273 kmh / 170 mph

Junkers W 33 and W 34

Close relatives of the very first all-metal transport monoplane, the Junkers F13, the W 33 and W 34 were developed concurrently in 1926 on the same production line as the F13, or so legend would have it. Differing from the F13 by virtue of a fuselage with greatly enlarged capacity, greater engine power and a modified wing planform, the W 33 was a dedicated freighter with a 170 cubic foot cargo hold, while the W 34 was an airliner with accommodation for six passengers and two crew. In the early versions, the crew sat in an open cockpit, but the cabin was always totally enclosed. Most versions of the W 33 used in-line Junkers engines, while the W 34 used a variety of radials. Featuring the same rugged corrugated aluminium skinning which characterised the F13, both versions were widely exported in the years before World War 2. Built in both land and seaplane versions, the W 33 saw extensive overseas service with operators in such far-flung places as China, Canada and New Guinea and inaugurated Lufthansa's regular mail services. Only a few examples of the W 33 survived to see service in the Luftwaffe, that service generally preferring the W 34, probably on account of the more reliable radial engine fitted to the W 34.

Likewise, the W 34 was built in numerous versions from 1927 onwards, the first production W 34b's being D-1119 and D-1294. Airline operators using the W 34 were Eurasia in China, Lloyd Aero in Bolivia, Guinea Airways in New Guinea and several Canadian companies. Later developments of the basic design had enclosed cockpits for the crew, and two of these, the W 34hau with a 650 hp BMW Bramo 322 engine driving a four-bladed wooden propeller and the W 34hi powered by a 660 hp BMW 132A and two-blade propeller, both saw extensive service in the Luftwaffe training schools throughout World War 2. About 100 examples of the W 34 are believed to have been built, the last in Sweden in 1935. For a time the W 34 was standard Luftwaffe equipment, with spartan accommodation for up to twelve passengers, for advanced flight training, blind flying training and radio operator instruction.

77: One of the rarer types of aircraft in service with the Luftwaffe 'B' and 'C' flying schools, a Junkers W33. ?K+AP may possibly be Werk Nummer 2517, the last two digits of which are just visible on the rudder balance. If this is correct, then this machine had a very long life, being first registered as D-1384 in June 1928, and serving variously with Severa, DLH, the DVL and DVS. The dark shield shape just behind the cockpit window may be the insignia of A/B 32, based at Chrudim, Czechoslovakia, February 1941

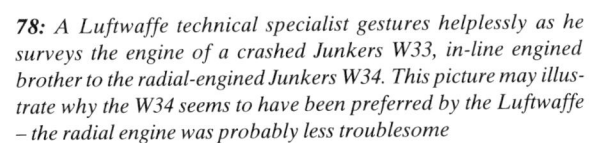

78: A Luftwaffe technical specialist gestures helplessly as he surveys the engine of a crashed Junkers W33, in-line engined brother to the radial-engined Junkers W34. This picture may illustrate why the W34 seems to have been preferred by the Luftwaffe – the radial engine was probably less troublesome

79: Luftwaffe aircrew trainees learning some of the finer points of hand-crank starting the BMW radial engine of a Junkers W34hau. Both this and the adjacent picture show machines in service with A/B 9 at Grottkau, probably in winter 1940-41. A/B 9 is unusual among Luftwaffe flying schools as it seems to have never used a unit badge

80: Pilot's view of the cockpit of a Junkers W34, probably the -hi version. There was a good deal of variation in the layout and number of the instruments in these types, depending on whether the particular aircraft was used for blind-flying, radio or navigational instruction etc.

81: An overall grey Junkers W34hau, probably from FFS A/B 13, ploughs through the slush on the airfield at Pilsen in Czechoslovakia

82: Junkers W34hau, BO+C/G/O/M. Exact date, location and owner uncertain, but provisionally identified as A/B 121, based at Straubing in Bavaria in mid-1940 (AMC)

83: Henschel Hs 123, Werk Nummer 2732, KB+QA, white '8', in service with an unidentified Stuka Vorschule. As was comon in the winter months, the wheel spats have been removed to avoid clogging with mud. The machine retains its original three tone upper surface camouflage (RLM 61/62/63). Note the feather edged finish to the dark green paint on the strut leading edge

84: View into a flying school-room, or what the student navigator or radio-operator saw in the cabin of the Junkers W34. The large hand-wheel at the top of the picture is for rotating the enormous external radio direction-finding loop which was such a prominent feature of the Junkers W34 types

85: Henschel Hs 123 in training school service. CA+AW, white '25', Werk Nummer 2303 was flown by August Diemer at Stuka Vorschule 1, Bad Aibling 1940-41. Diemer later went on to complete over 600 operational missions with 8./St.G 77 on the Russian Front, Italy and in the Western Desert, winning the German Cross in Gold in the process. Note the 87 octane marking on the belly fuel tank and what appears to be a yellow underside to the engine cowling added to the original well-worn RLM 61/62/63 camouflage (AMC)

86: Another view of Henschel Hs 123, CA+AW, white '25', seen also in photo 85. Stuka Vorschule 1, Bad Aibling, summer 1941 (AMC)

87: Another elderly Henschel Hs 123, BQ+NL, Werk Nummer 2729, seen in service in winter 1939-40 with an unidentified Luftwaffe training school. Location is probably somewhere in occupied Czechoslovakia. Note how on this aircraft the code is carried on the underside of the lower wing, as opposed to the upper wing as seen in photo 86

88: A well known Junkers Ju 87A, ??+BV, yellow '6', Werk No. 5040, named 'Irene'. What is not so well known is that the pilot was August Diemer, an instructor at Stuka Vorschule 1, whose girlfriend was called Irene. Note the yellow underside wingtips. Bad Aibling, winter 1940-41. The school was later transferred to San Damiano in Italy and re-numbered Stuka Vorschule 3 (AMC)

Despite being generally well behaved in the air, the marginal centre of gravity of the W 34 could give rise to some interesting moments on the landing run, and too-hasty application of the brakes frequently tipped the bird onto its nose. Units known to have operated the W 34 include FFS A/B 2, FFS A/B 5, FFS A/B 11, FFS A/B 14, FFS A 32, FFS B 1, FFS (C)3, BFS 33 and LKS 13. Data for the W 34hi landplane:

Span:	17.75m / 58 ft 2 3/4 in)
Length:	10.27m / 33 ft 8 in)
Weight:	3200 kg / 7056 lb (Fully loaded)
Max Speed:	265 kmh / 165 mph

Caudron C.445 *Göeland* (Seagull)

A twin-engined low wing monoplane with accommodation for up to six passengers and a crew of two, the Göeland was one of the most successful products of the French Caudron company in the interwar period. Built almost entirely of wood except for the aluminium nose cone and the fabric covering to the fuselage sides, with an undercarriage which retracted into the engine nacelles, the prototype C.440 first flew in 1934. During the next three years the type proved to be an exceptional aircraft and gained acclaim in several air races.

Several versions of the Göeland were built, essentially differing only in the degree of wing dihedral and the engine installation. An interesting point about the type is that the engines both rotated outwards, thereby cancelling out torque effects. So far as is known all aircraft were fitted with one type of Renault inline engine or another; the C.445M trainer, produced for the Armée de l'Air, being powered by a pair of 220 hp Renault 6 Pdi's. After the occupation of France, production continued for both the Vichy government and the Luftwaffe. Most wartime models were built by Renault at their Billancourt plant. Little is known about the C.445 in Luftwaffe service, although large numbers were produced for them, FFS B 20 being one known user. Production continued post-war and eventually some 1,702 were built.

Span:	17.60m / 57 ft 9 in)
Length:	13.80m / 45 ft 3 3/4 in)
Weight:	3500 kg / 7700 lb (Fully loaded)
Max Speed:	300 kmh / 186 mph

Miscellaneous Schools

Other, more highly specialised training units existed in the Luftwaffe, as in other air forces, yet very little seems to have been recorded about their activities. In the hope that more information may be forthcoming some of those known are listed in *Table 16*:

Table 16

Bordfunkerschule Halle/Saale – Radio Operator School Based Halle/Saale. Linked with LKS 13?

Flugzeugführerüberprüfungsschule – Aircrew Check-out Unit. Based Prenzlau, Pasewalk, Salzwedel

Fluglehrschule der Luftwaffe – Flying Instructors School Based Brandenburg-Briest. Some aircraft taken over by JV 44 in 1945

Ergänzungsgruppe (S) 1 –
Primary and operational training for assault and cargo glider pilots (S=Schlepp i.e. towed).
Based Langendiebach, near Hanau 1942-43

Erg.Gr.(S) 1 used a variety of glider types and some exotic tug aircraft. These included about ten ex-Latvian Air Force Gloster Gladiators, captured from the Russians in 1941. Known codes include 1E+PH, 1E+SH, 1E+DK, 1E+BL, 1E+JM and NJ+BO.

As is well known, the Luftwaffe made extensive use of gliders throughout the war. Unlike the Allied forces, German glider pilots and paratroops were a part of the air force, consequently it was far easier to integrate the glider-borne assault troops and subsequent supply missions into air-landing operations. Training of the large number of glider pilots required was facilitated by the basic air experience given within the ranks of the Hitler Youth and NSFK.

It is not proposed to go into great detail here concerning the many different types of gliders used within the para-military Nazi youth training organisations, suffice it to say that primary training was usually carried out on the Grunau 9, the notorious 'Skull-splitter', and the NSFK's own SG38. This was followed by more sophisticated types such as the Grunau Baby, DFS Olympia and Göppingen Minimoa. By the time a student had gained his civil gliding proficiency 'C' Certificate, he was already a capable pilot. (The NSFK also offered a powered aircraft pilot's licence. This, however, did not spare the holder from a single hour of instruction with the Luftwaffe, as the NSFK award was not recognised by the Luftwaffe!) The essential role of the Luftwaffe glider training schools therefore was to ensure that he was capable of flying and landing the heavy Luftwaffe gliders in combat conditions.

One other unit, unique to the Luftwaffe, was the *Lehrgeschwader* – Training Division. The need to evaluate new types of aircraft, equipment and tactics led to the establishment of a *Lehrgruppe* in Greifswald in 1936. Essentially, this consisted of a number of small units representative of the many kinds of flying units within the Luftwaffe formed into a larger size which simplified administration, but also allowed different combinations of equipment and tactics to be tried out.

Examples of every item of equipment used by the Luftwaffe were delivered for testing to the Lehrgruppe, which worked in close co-operation with the RLM and the various test facilities such as Rechlin and Travemünde. Results from these experiments were then fed back into the Luftwaffe operational and training units. Eventually, the favourable experience obtained with this unit and the rapid expansion of the Luftwaffe led to two complete Geschwader being in existence by the outbreak of war, being made up as shown in *Table 17*:

Table 17	
Lehrgeschwader 1	
Geschwaderstab/LG 1	Greifswald
I.(Schw. Jagd)/LG 1	Barth – Heavy Fighters
II.(Kampf)/LG 1	Schwerin – Bombers
III.(Kampf)/LG 1	Greifswald – Bombers
IV.(Stuka)/LG 1	Barth – Dive Bombers
Lehrgeschwader 2	
Geschwaderstab/LG 2	Garz
I.(Jagd)/LG 2	Garz – Fighters
II.(Schlacht)/LG2	Tutow – Ground Attack
III.(Aufkl.)/LG 2	Jüterbog – Reconnaissance
10.(See)/LG 2	Travemünde – Marine
11.(NJ)/LG 2	Garz – Nightfighters

There was also a third such unit, LG3, which had only a brief existence between December 1939 and February 1940. It then formed the nucleus of KG 1.

Perfectly capable of mounting actual operations, LG 1 in particular gained an enviable war record in its own right, possibly at the expense of its intended purpose as an evaluation unit.

Sea Eagles

One of the many organisational anomalies in the Nazi armed forces was that of the small naval air arm – the *Seeluftstreitkräfte*. In a not dissimilar structure to the pre-war Fleet Air Arm of the Royal Navy, the actual units were under the command of a Luftwaffe general – the *General der Luftwaffe beim Oberkommando der Kriegsmarine* – Ob.d.M. for short, who in turn reported to the Naval High Command. As the RAF and Royal Navy also found, this arrangement gave ample opportunities for friction and confusion between the two services.

In the absence of shipborne radar or aircraft carriers, the Kriegsmarine regarded the primary purpose of naval air power to be that of maritime reconnaissance and occasional mine-laying and torpedo bombing. The designations of the operational maritime units – the *Küstenfliegergruppen* – reflected the primarily coastal nature of their duties. In any case, only the larger German naval vessels were capable of carrying aircraft, and these were only two-seat floatplanes suitable for short-range duties. The longer distance search operations were to be carried out by land-based flying boats, attack capability generally resting with the He 115 floatplanes or land-based bombers. By 1943 most of the naval units had been absorbed into the Luftwaffe proper.

Lack of overwater navigational experience on the part of the Luftwaffe resulted in a similar situation to that of the British Fleet Air Arm in the years preceding World War II whereby most of the members of the crews in the maritime units were from the air force, but navigators and observers were naval personnel. Training was therefore geared to these ends. The specialist nature of marine air warfare, particularly the late development of aerial torpedo attacks upon shipping, led to the logical decision to base the *Flugzeugführerschulen (See)* – marine pilot training schools – around the pre-war experimental and

89: An elderly Junkers Ju 87A-2. This may be TY+NV, in use as a trainer with SG 102 at Deutsches-Brod in Czechoslovakia in summer 1944. The faint outline of a shield-shaped unit emblem can be just made out above the wing leading edge

testing stations on the Baltic coast at Warnemünde, Pütnitz and Stettin. For a short time there was also a maritime aircrew replacement pool, the *Flieger-Ergänzungsgruppe (See)*, based at Kamp in Pomerania. Associated with the specialist training of naval aviators were three *Fliegerwaffenschulen* (See) – naval aviation weapons schools i.e. OTUs. On 1st September 1939 these were as shown in *Table 18*.

Main aircraft equipment for the C2 advanced marine schools was usually an assortment of Dornier Wal and Do 18 flying boats and He 59, He 60 and He 115 floatplanes, although a few floatplane variants of the Ju 52/3m and Ju W 34 also saw service.

Table 18

Fliegerwaffenschulen (See)

Unit	Date Formed	Main Bases Used	Comments
FWS (See) 1	1934	Parow	Originally DVS at Warnemünde
FWS (See) 2	1934	Bug am Rügen	So named in 1939
FWS (See) 3	1939	Dievenow	Transferred from Warnemünde

90: Starboard side view of one of the rarer aircraft to see service in the Luftwaffe – a Junkers Ju 160, registration WL-URIF. In theory this should date the picture to no later than October 1939 when the WL- prefix was dropped, although it was far from uncommon for aircraft in training schools to retain obsolete markings for months, if not years. According to the caption on the back of the original picture, the location was Warsaw. About sixty of these aircraft were completed, some 21 seeing service with Lufthansa, but they were not particularly successful

91: A very rare bird. Messerschmitt M20b, WL-UKUM, in Luftwaffe service. The aircraft still retains the logo of its previous owner, Hansa Luftdienst, the ancestor of DLH. First entering service in 1931, this aircraft, Werk Nummer 542, was originally registered D-2025. Re-registered D-UKUM and named 'Westerwald' in 1933, in 1939 it acquired the WL- trainer code as shown here. The rudder and fin have been overpainted, possibly in yellow, but the red stripe behind the swastika still shows through. WL-UKUM was destroyed in 1942 (AMC?)

THE WINGS ARE CLIPPED
Courage is not enough

"The training for the blind-flying 'C' pilot's licence was the longest, most costly, most complicated, and from the point of view of wartime operational effectiveness, most important aspect of the entire air training process" – Generalleutnant Werner Kreipe

At the outbreak of the war, there were some 1,505 bombers, 1,325 fighters, 620 reconnaissance machines, 205 seaplanes and 450 transport aircraft in service with the Luftwaffe. Another 1,500 crews were under training in the weapons schools, so that there were about 5,000 crews available, representing some 15,000 men.

Belated recognition by the Luftwaffe General Staff that the war situation in early 1943 had finally forced the Luftwaffe to become a defensive, rather than an offensive force, led to the start of a fundamental shift in the composition of the organisation. Despite stubborn resistance by Hitler to acknowledge the reality of the position, the more clear-sighted Luftwaffe commanders had seen the need for change in both tactics, aircraft production and the training of crews for these machines. Subsequently, the appointment of *Generalleutnant* Werner Kreipe as Chief of Training in June 1943, and the wholesale re-appraisal of the training units which followed in October, led to a doubling in the output of crews by the beginning of 1944, despite a 20% drop in the number of basic personnel. Not only this, but more modern aircraft had at last begun to reach the training units in 1943, with nearly 1,000 Fw 190 and Bf 109 fighters available in the fighter schools by late 1944. An indication of the shift in emphasis in the offensive/defensive capability of the Luftwaffe is reflected in the number and type of crews qualifying in 1942-43:

Crews	1942	1943
Bomber	1,962	3,231
Day Fighter	1,662	3,276
Night Fighter	239	1,358
Ground Attack		5371,264
Reconnaissance		192464

By 1943-44 the Luftwaffe had reached its maximum size with 2,089,000 men under arms. There were, however, several negative aspects to this apparently encouraging picture. Instructors remained in short supply and were a source of constant worry to *Generalleutnant* Adolf Galland, chief of the fighter arm, who was highly critical of the lack of long term planning responsible for such a situation. There was a lack of co-ordination between the schools and the operational units which meant that pilots would find different practices at the squadrons to those which they had been taught, and the lack of flying time

92: Crashlanded Junkers Ju 86E, ??+PX, still wearing the pre-war three-colour camouflage scheme. The barely discernible emblem under the cockpit may be that of FFS (C) 22. Location is believed to be Prague-Ruzyne. Note the Lufthansa hangar in the background and and two more Ju 86 aircraft (Richard L. Ward)

meant that many pilots were still pre-occupied with the technicalities of flying when they arrived at their operational units.

Increasing demands from the battle fronts meant that by 1944 turnover of aircrew was such that in many units only the Gruppe and Staffel commanders had more than six months experience, while the majority of pilots had only seen active service for some 8 to 30 *days*. Not only this, but in order to achieve the required numbers of new pilots, their training had had to be drastically reduced with a consequent deterioration in quality. This was compounded by 'surplus' ground personnel being drafted willy-nilly into the army or Luftwaffe ground formations to shore up crumbling infantry regiments, consequently aircraft maintenance and serviceability also suffered. This was the situation in February 1944, when German plans to remedy the situation were abruptly and violently overturned.

First there was a renewed Allied bomber offensive aimed specifically at German aircraft production facilities – 23 airframe and 3 engine factories being attacked in that month. Even worse, the daylight bombers were accompanied all the way to the targets and back by long-range fighters. The shock to the German defence systems that this represented was enormous. Indeed, until the previous winter, the research branch of the RLM had been claiming that such a machine was a technical impossibility! At one stroke, all existing German plans for aircraft production and training were thrown into disarray. With the ability to strike almost at will anywhere within the Reich, the arrival of the American escort fighters was to prove a mortal blow.

Subject to the debilitating personality conflicts within the higher echelons of the Luftwaffe command, beset by growing shortages of fuel and instructors, forced into constant moves by the shrinking perimeters of the Reich and now no longer safe even on its own airfields, the training system was no longer capable of allowing the Luftwaffe to recuperate its strength. It was the beginning of the end.

Ironically, by January 1945, the numbers of Luftwaffe flying personnel had reached an all-time high of 26,411 officers and 632,486 NCOs qualified as aircrew. The numbers were there, but not the vital element of quality. Products of the reduced standards of training prevailing at that stage of the war, these men were greatly inferior in terms of skill compared to those of the victorious air force of spring 1940, yet they were no less courageous.

Generalfeldmarschall Erhard Milch may have overstated the case when he claimed that "the Luftwaffe training programme, and with it the Luftwaffe itself, was throttled to death by the fuel shortage," but there can be no arguing with the fact that between 1 September 1939 and 31 December 1944, 9,521 would-be airmen had been killed in training, while 5,993 were injured. Another 81,403 were killed, wounded or went missing on operations – all for the sake of a madman's twisted dream.

Markings & Camouflage

In the days before the Luftwaffe officially emerged into the daylight, all aircraft in service were classified as 'civilian'. From 20 March 1934, after the Nazi Party had gained power, the civil registration system was extensively revised. Previously, aircraft were identified by a combination letter/number code. For instance, a BFW M.23b light floatplane belonging to the Messerschmitt factory in 1930 was registered D-1836 and an early Heinkel He 60B in service with the *RDL Erprobungstelle Travemünde* was registered D-2325. 'D' of course identified 'Deutschland'. The new system introduced by the Nazis consisted of the D- prefix followed by a four letter combination and was discussed earlier. This system prevailed until the spring of 1936 when the first of a rapid series of changes took place.

Aircraft in service with first-line units began to display a narrow straight-sided cross, similar to that used in late 1918, inserted into the registration letters on the fuselage and at the end of the registration on the wings. Needless to say, this resulted in some very crowded lettering. By June, further revisions took place. The first was the mandatory display of the *hakenkreuz* or swastika on both sides of the fin instead of only on the port side as previously. This was in black on a white disc, centred on a red band and applied to all aircraft.

The other change was the use of military codes using letter/number combinations. It is not proposed to discuss how these new regulations effected operational machines here, only those in use as trainers. Essentially, the code consisted of five or six digits, the first of which was the letter 'S' to signify school. This system appears to have been restricted to ex-operational aircraft relegated to training duties, not to aircraft specifically designed for that task. For example, an Arado Ar 68E in use as a fighter trainer with the code S3+R01 which can be broken down as follows:

S	= *Schule* (School)
3	= *Luftkreis* (Air District)
+	
R	= Staffel or flight in school (or possibly school within the Luftkreis)
01	= identity of aircraft within the school

The large numbers of aircraft allocated to each school, of which there were several in each Luftkreis, could have easily used up all available letters, so it is this writer's belief that the second letter may in fact have served to identify the school.

Until January 1939, dedicated unarmed training aircraft used purely civil registrations. From that date, the D- prefix was supposed to have been deleted and substituted by the letters WL *(Wehrmacht Luft)*. The difficulties in applying this change to large numbers of aircraft can be imagined. The outbreak of war in September 1939 resulted in an order to apply the *Balkenkreuz* (bar cross) to all military aircraft. In many cases there was simply no room – the hyphen dividing the WL from the other four letters was therefore used as a basis for a cross.

Change quickly followed change, when the WL registrations were abolished in October 1939 in favour of the simpler system which was to endure for the rest of the war. This consisted of four letters running in alphabetical sequence from and gave an enormous number of potential combinations. Essentially, the system ran in alphabetical progression i.e. AA+AA to AA+AZ, then AA+BA to AA+BZ, and so on. Both manufacturers and training units were allocated blocks of letters, among which were gaps for security purposes. These letters were almost invariably painted in black on the fuselage sides and underwing. When dark upper surfaces began to appear later in the war, the fuselage letters were frequently thinly outlined in white.

In the early days, the first two letters sometimes served to identify units. For instance, PF+?? is believed to have identified aircraft based on the group of airfields to the west of Prague in Czechoslovakia. As new aircraft were delivered or transferred, however, codes became inevitably mixed. In many instances, the third letter may also have served to identify the staffel or flight to which the aircraft belonged, the last letter being the individual aircraft itself. For example, a number of Klemm Kl 25 aircraft based at Marienbad in 1940-41 all carried the code PF+V?, while others of the same type bore the code PF+W?. Unfortunately, this theory is complicated by the sequential letter groupings issued to many manufacturers, such as the batch of Arado Ar 96's which included the codes GV+CE, GV+CI, GV+CV etc. Much research is still needed here.

A simpler means of identification was often seen on aircraft on training airfields later in the war. This was simply a prominently sized number, often of three digits, usually painted in white or yellow on some convenient surface of the aircraft such as nose or tail. These were probably given to individual aircraft on an airfield without regard to type. JFS 1 at Werneuchen had used a similar system in 1939 when the complex nature of the quasi-civil 'WL-' letter codes led to demands for a simpler system of identification. Every aircraft on the base received an individual number, and on the evidence of several photos it seems that the Fw 56 types received a yellow (or possibly white) band with black numbers, while the Ar 68's received a red band with white numbers. This system was not necessarily applied at other bases.

Training aircraft also carried the same range of crosses and swastikas as worn by other machines. These varied from extra large wing crosses of the early war period to the white outline only type seen much later in the war, although many training machines existed for years in their original finish. Indeed, at least one Klemm Kl 25, D-ENAA, survived to be captured in 1945 still in its original pre-war silver dope and civilian markings. Czech aircraft in Luftwaffe training service in particular seem to have often carried swastikas of gigantic proportions across the entire vertical tail surfaces.

A less obvious marking, but one frequently seen on machines during the early part of the war was a small data table, usually near the tail of the aircraft, which gave the type of aircraft and the address and telephone number of the training school to which it was attached – a useful feature in the event of forced landings away from base!

Special markings were carried by some aircraft. Those in use as blind-flying trainers carried double yellow bands around the fuselage, while the Bü 133 types often retained a spectacular white-outlined green (*not* red) flash down their fuselage sides. Another infrequently seen device was a narrow-based inverted red triangle with a whiteoutline which was applied to the fuselage side with the point at the leading edge of the wings. This is believed to have served as a 'beware propeller' safety marking.

Finally, most, but not all, flying schools had their unit emblem which was painted on many aircraft, even late in the war when conditions for training were very difficult. The colour illustrations in this book show all those known at the time of writing.

Colours

As might be expected, Luftwaffe trainers followed the general rules regarding painting, but had no special camouflage. In view of the enormous drain on resources involved in repainting aircraft, trainers could be seen in their original paint schemes long after they were first built.

In the early days, all aircraft were finished in aluminium-silver dope (RLM 01), often with the fuselage spine painted in dark blue or green as an anti-glare measure. An example is an Fw 44, D-EVYM, in service with an unknown unit in 1936. Later deliveries were more usually finished in the standard all-purpose greenish-grey, RLM 02 or RLM 63, often with a glossy appearance. Bücker types were most frequently finished in a light *'Perle-weiss'* – pearl-grey – colour as a standard factory scheme, at least in the pre-war days. A single overall colour remained the standard finish until increasing numbers of Allied fighters began to make life dangerous for the trainees. Orders were issued that from 21 January

93: A Czech-built Aero Ab 101 bomber believed to be in service with FFS A/B 13, probably for air-gunnery training. The enormous size of this ponderous biplane is immediately apparent from the scale of the man standing in front of the wing root. Pilsen in Czechoslovakia.

94 Below: Ground crewmen use an hydraulic loading trolley to hoist a bomb onto the port wing root rack of a Junkers Ju 88A which carries the Pomeranian griffin (greif) insignia of LG 1. Location is Greifswald, hence the probable inspiration for the badge

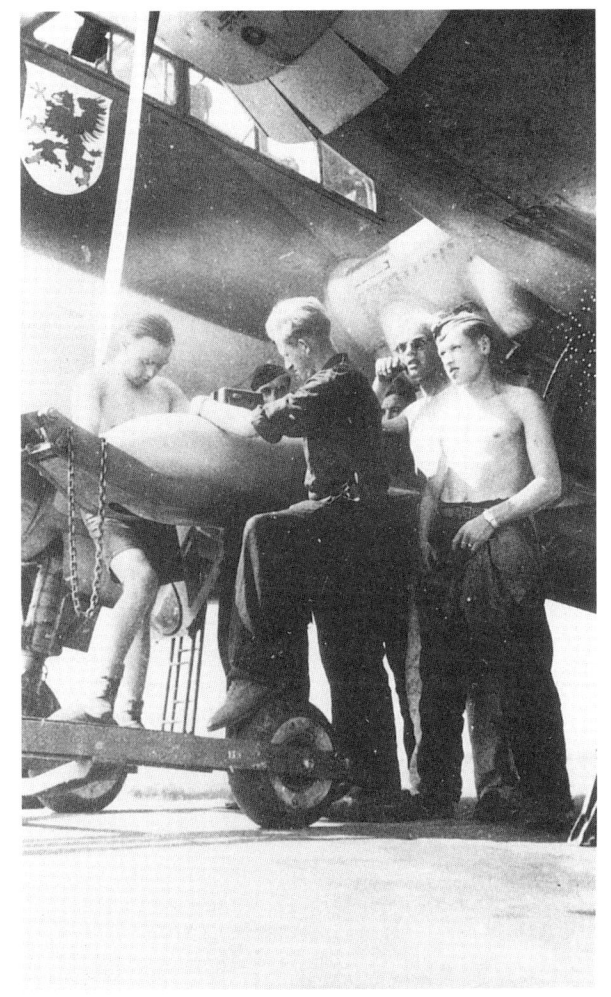

1942, all training aircraft finished in light colours were to receive an overall coat of a dark green, 70 or 71, on the upper surfaces, to serve as camouflage, both in the air and on the ground. With the advent of the darker finishes, yellow bands, wingtips, rudders or cowlings similar to those used on the Eastern Front were applied for safety reasons.

Obsolescent aircraft relegated to training rarely changed their operational colour schemes except where necessary to carry their new unit markings. The result was an often amazing variety of colour schemes on a training airfield. Study of the colour illustrations in this book shows just a few!

As the net tightened around Germany, there arose a general need for quick identification markings. Consequently, an order on 20 July 1944 required that all fighters, ground attack and reconnaissance machines were to carry a white spiral on black propeller spinners; captured aircraft were also to carry this marking and the wing undersurfaces inboard from the tips painted yellow to an amount equal to one-third of the span. Civil aircraft were to receive yellow paint under the fuselage, on the whole of the engine cowlings and the rudder. With the intensifying air war over Germany, however, the distinction between civil and military aircraft became increasingly blurred and it is probable that the yellow underside to the fuselage was only applied in exceptional cases. With the exception of the yellow fuselage undersurface this scheme resembled that worn by many trainers. Captured enemy aircraft in use as trainers almost invariably received an overall coat of yellow (RLM 04) on their undersurfaces to identify them as 'friendly', although as ever with the Luftwaffe, there were many exceptions to the rule.

95: *A Dornier Do 23, S6+C97, aircraft '97' of 'C' flight of a School attached to Luftkreis 6. An interesting affiliation as Luftkreis 6 was essentially concerned with marine aviation activities along the Baltic coast. A Junkers W 34, rudderless He 70 and He 50 can be seen in the background. Finish is probably overall RLM 02 Grau (AMC)*

96: *An overall dark green Caudron C445 in Luftwaffe service. Over 1200 of these light twins were produced both before, during and after the war, and saw extensive service with the Luftwaffe as trainers, communication and ambulance aircraft. The example here, DS+?? is in full Luftwaffe camouflage and markings in service with an unknown unit*

97: *Crashlanded Dornier Do 17E, BA+DX. This one is actually in service with the Luftdienst, whose blue and yellow triangular insignia can be seen under the cockpit, but the aircraft is typical of many used in the training schools. Camouflage scheme is still the pre-war RLM 61/62/63 scheme. 1st May 1941, location unknown, possibly Czechoslovakia (R.L. Ward)*

98: A good closeup of the nose of a Junkers Ju 52/3m of FFS(C) 15, a training unit based at Avord, near Bourges, in France from January 1943 for the training of Heinkel He 177 heavy bomber crews. The white number 19 just below the cockpit probably identifies the number of the aircraft in the unit (AMC)

99: An immaculate Heinkel He 60, D-IVKA, tied up to the slipway at Bug am Rügen, home of Fliegerwaffenschule (See) in July 1936. Finish is probably the standard for the type at the time – overall RLM 02 Grau with silver floats

100: Dornier Do 16 Wal D-ABAU, the militarised version of the famous Dornier Do J IId. Note the three machine gun positions, the one at the nearside rear fuselage being occupied by a shy crew member. The maritime reconnaissance units based at List and equipped with the Wal went through a bewildering variety of designations. First formed as 1.(Mz)/186 on 1 October 1934, by late 1936 they were known as 2.(F)/106. Eventually the remaining Wals were passed on to the maritime training units (AMC)

Captions to Colour Illustrations

Page 41

1: Klemm L25, D-EQIP, is typical of the innocent small aircraft on which many a Luftwaffe fighter ace cut his teeth. Shown as it appeared when it served with the para-military NSFK flying school at Herzogenaurach in 1937, it is finished in an attractive mix of clear varnished ply and silver doped fabric, the engine cowling being left in its natural aluminium colour. Note the NSFK emblem just below the forward cockpit.

2: Klemm L25, PF+VN, shows the later all-silver finish used extensively on primary training aircraft. It is seen here as it appeared during its service with A/B 8 at Marienbad in Czechoslovakia in 1940-41. This is confirmed by Unteroffizier Bruno Pacher's logbook which records that he flew in it four times on 10 January 1941. The Werk Nummer may have been 256 or 267.

3: Bücker Bü 131, CW+BG, Werk Nummer 483, was flown by a pupil from A 43 at Crailsheim, who landed at Basle, Switzerland, on 14 June 1944, having mistaken the city for Strassburg. Finished in overall RLM 71 Dunkelgrün with RLM 65 undersides, the machine is a classic example of a late-war trainer. It is exceptionally fully marked by virtue of its unit emblem, school number (50) and white outlined Stammkenzeichen fuselage codes and fuselage crosses. The German pilot expressed a preference for internment and the aircraft was consequently flown back to Freiburg by a Swiss pilot.

4: The Bücker Bü 131 served other masters as well as the Luftwaffe. This overall RLM 02 Grüngrau machine served as a trainer, courier and liaison machine with the Hungarian III. Közelfelderítő század – III. Tactical Reconnaissance squadron – whose falcon emblem can be seen on the fuselage. Note the chevron-style national markings used only until 1 March 1942. The original picture on which this illustration is based does not show the code absolutely clearly, but notes that the serial number is I-333, as shown. This is of interest as it is outside the range of numbers officially allocated to the type. This could mean therefore that the serial is actually I-233. Photographic evidence exists, however, for other out-of-sequence numbers for the type in Hungarian service, possibly indicating that those machines were impressed civilian aircraft.

5: Not only heavy aircraft were taken from the training schools for service on the Eastern Front. Klemm Kl 35D, DL+UI, Werk Nummer 3198, was detached from LKS 3 at Wildpark-Werder for temporary service as a courier, hence the winter camouflage.

6: Overall RLM 02 Klemm Kl 35B, Werk Nummer 1416, PT+NY, showing the famous 'Detmold swimming trunks' emblem of A/B 113.

7: Bücker Bü 181, GL+SU, of A/B 115, based at Wels, is an unusually colourful example of the breed. Most were fairly anonymous, but in addition to the typical later style of white-outlined code letters and aircraft-in-school number, this aircraft also wears the two yellow bands indicative of a blind-flying trainer. Apart from the school emblem (a visual pun, a katzenwels being a catfish in German), the small number '6' is also recorded as being an alternative school insignia.

Page 42

8: 3 view of Klemm Kl 35D, NQ+NR, in overall RLM 02 Grüngrau from A/B 71 based at Prossnitz sometime in 1941.

9: 3 view of Bücker Bü 131, TA+AH, red '102' in what was probably the most common finish of the type – overall RLM 02.

Page 43

10: TA+KK is an ex-Armée de l'Air North American NA 57, in use by JVS 3 based at Vienna-Schwechat. Note the unpainted rear canopy frame and panelling. The Luftwaffe also took over considerable numbers of NA 64s from the French.

11: All-silver Focke-Wulf Fw 44F, KJ+OE, of A/B 23 at Kaufbeuren, sometime in 1940.

12: Praga E39, construction number 18, (just visible above the unit badge of A/B 32). VB+SI was one of the standard Czech air force trainers at the time of the German takeover and large numbers were absorbed into the Luftwaffe. Location is Pardubitz (now Pardubice) in Czechoslovakia, probably in 1940. Many of these aircraft carried their call signs on the upper surface of the top wing.

13: Heinkel He 72, BO+BY, Werk Nummer 472, wearing a weathered silver finish and skis was used as a glider tug by A/B 5 at Seerappen, near Königsberg in East Prussia during 1940-41.

14: Arado Ar 66, NG+MY, Werk Nummer 873, reveals the temporary night camouflage hastily applied to many such aircraft pressed into service for night harassment duties on the Eastern Front.

15: Gotha Go 145, TD+BA, Werk Nummer 1258, was one of several captured by British forces at the end of the war. Wearing what appears to be a dense green mottle over the basic RLM 02 finish, it has been fitted with a replacement rudder. It has also been converted into a blind-flying trainer by the simple expedient of a cover over the rear cockpit. Crosses on the wings were of the outline only type.

Page 44

16: 3 view of Focke-Wulf Fw 44F, TW+NO, of A/B 112, in what appears to be overall RLM 71 upper surfaces, with an unusually glossy finish. Undersides are probably RLM 65. The dark finish suggests that the aircraft was then probably based at Nellingen.

17: Gotha Go 145, SL+MV, wearing the seahorse badge of A/B 5. Originally based at Seerappen near Königsberg in East Prussia, the unit merged with A/B 33 in 1941, but was reformed as A5 in 1944 at Gablingen. The dark finish almost certainly dates the aircraft to this period.

18: Arado Ar 96B, NU+OL, of A/B 61. Finish is 70/71/65.

19:     Arado Ar 96B, yellow '254' of JFS 2, based at Magdeburg/Zerbst. It is painted in the early overall RLM 02 scheme except for the black panels, applied by tidy-minded ground crew, intended to hide the engine exhaust staining.

Page 45

20:     This Beneš-Mráz Be 51 'Beta Minor', GA+AB, was one of several Czech civilian types taken over by the Luftwaffe as useful trainers. The machine is depicted wearing a standard factory finish of light cream with black (possibly red) trim, with RLM 04 yellow engine cowling and rudder. A similar machine, without the yellow, was coded BZ+AV.

21:     Bücker Bü 133C, wearing the quasi-civil registration D-EGHV which was carried both above the top and below the lower wings. This was one of the NSFK Aerobatic Flight machines in 1939 and is finished in overall RLM 02. Frequently shown as red, the fuselage stripe was, in fact, green as illustrated. The purpose of the red disc is not known.

22:     D-IZAM is an Arado Ar 65 used by Leutnant Herwig Knüppels at the covert DVS fighter school at Schleißheim in 1935. Knüppels 'top hat' emblem is just visible below the windscreen. Something of a comedian, Knüppels took his "zylinder-hut" emblem to Spain, where it was adopted as the emblem of 2.J/88 during the Civil War and he became an ace. He was later killed in action in World War II.

23:     Messerschmitt Bf 109D-1, S2+M53, displays the short-lived school codes used by JFS 1 at Werneuchen immediately prior to the outbreak of war in 1939. Finish is the standard 70/71/65 of the period.

24:     Focke-Wulf Fw 56, RT+NP, in an attractive all-silver finish, belonged to A/B 4 based at Prague-Gbell in late 1939.

25:     Focke-Wulf Fw 56, BM+NW, looks quite menacing in its warpaint. The original caption to this picture indicates that the aircraft was in service with the advanced fighter trainer unit, Erg.J.Gr.Ost, based at Krakow in Poland, although the unit emblem is more commonly associated with EJG 1, in France.

Page 46

26:     Arado Ar 68E, VB+NQ, Werk Nummer 1558, is finished in a loose pattern of RLM 70 and 71 on the uppersurfaces and served with A/B 32 in Pardubitz in 1941. The significance of the white disc is not known, but it is unlikely to be an unfinished unit emblem as this was shield-shaped. Note the offset 'Q'.

27:     Heinkel He 51B, GU+NW, white '2', was probably finished in overall RLM 63. It served with an unidentified Jagdflieger Schule as an advanced fighter-trainer.

28:     Arado Ar 68E, S7+S33, finished in overall RLM 02, shows by its 'S7' code that it was in service with a training school in Luftkreis 7, namely the Aufklärungsfliegerschule Brieg in Silesia in winter 1939-40.

29:     This all-silver Czech-built Avia Ba 122 served as an aerobatic trainer with A/B 4 at Prague-Gbell during spring 1941.

30:     Luftwaffe use of captured Soviet aircraft is not well recorded, although a sizeable number did reach the training schools in 1941-42. This is a Yakovlev UTI, which served in the Soviet VVS as as the standard advanced trainer for fighter pilots. The silver and red scheme is as captured except for the addition of German markings and yellow theatre bands.

31:     A most unusual type in German service. Once a frontline Soviet fighter, this is a Polikarpov I-153 used by JVS 3 in Vienna-Schwechat as an advanced fighter-trainer. Finish is overall RLM 02.

Page 47

32:     Morane-Saulnier MS 406, TP+ZM, seen here in service with JG 103 at Chateauroux in France. Finish is believed to be RLM 74/75/76 with large areas of yellow as shown.

33:     Dewoitine D.520, NE+GZ, yellow '94', in use as an advanced trainer with JG 101 at Pau, France. It is shown here in standard Luftwaffe day fighter colours of 74/75/76, but interpretation of black and white pictures being what it is...

34:     Morane-Saulnier MS230 Et, construction number 836, is believed to have carried the French matricule militaire M94. Most examples captured went to the Luftwaffe training schools, but this one was one of five used for testing at Brandenburg-Briest in late 1940.

35:     Arado Ar 68F, PX+NQ, was used by A/B 32 for advanced pilot training at their base at Pardubitz in Czechoslovakia. Alfred Aurass was one student to fly it in August 1942. Note the massive engine exhausts.

36:     Messerschmitt Bf 109G-12, yellow '27' of JG 101 at Pau, France in March 1944. This aircraft was probably converted from a G-4 fighter. The remains of the Stammkennzeichen, BJ+DZ, can still be seen. Note the difference in size between the letters.

37:     Messerschmitt Bf 109E, Red '7' of II./EJG 3 finished in 71/02/65. This aircraft was damaged during a landing attempt at Krakow, Poland, when it collided with a Junkers Ju 52/3m of FFS (C) 17.

Page 48

38:     Messerchmitt Bf 109G-12/R-3, black '512', converted from a G-4, in service with an unidentified advanced fighter school.

39:     Focke-Wulf Fw 190S-8, (S = 'Schule'), red '55', belonging to an unidentified advanced fighter school.

40:     Focke-Wulf Fw 190S-5, GO+MV, in typically nondescript finish. Unit unknown.

41:     Messerschmitt Me 262B-1a, white '35', Werk Nummer 110639 (incorrectly shown as 110689) was one of about fifteen of the type which actually found their way into service. Converted into a two-seater by Blohm & Voss at Wenzendorfer in summer 1944, it was employed by III./EJG 2 at Lager-Lechfeld. Finished in an uneven mottle of (probably) RLM 81 and 82 over 76 undersurfaces. The front of the engine cowlings are in silver to denote the aircraft's trainer status. It is also possible that the outer third of the starboard wing was painted white, although whether this was applied before or after its capture by the Americans is unknown. The machine is currently serving as a pattern aircraft for a small production run of new-build (!) Me 262s in Texas.

42:    DB+YG is an Heinkel He 45 in service with the Aufklärungsfliegerschule at Brieg in Silesia in February 1940. Large areas of RLM 70 and 71 have been sprayed over the basic RLM 02 finish. Note how the original red tail band still shows through the overspray of 02.

43:    This Heinkel He 46 wears the usual pre-war camouflage pattern of RLM 61/62/63 with 65 undersurfaces. Clearly marked with the 'school' codes S2+A35 denoting ownership by Luftkreis 2, it was in use by the the flying school of FAR 22 in Neustadt-Glewe in August 1939.

Page 49

44:    Henschel Hs 123A, PF+UV, white '7', was one of twelve in use as operational trainers by Erg./SG 1 at Novotscherkask in Russia in 1941-42. Still finished in the pre-war three-tone camouflage scheme of RLM 61/62/63 with 65 undersurfaces, the colours have been applied in an interesting variation to standard, although the pattern remains the same. It has been touched over where the fuselage codes have been applied. Note that the code was carried under the upperwing inboard of the main struts.

45:    Heinkel He 50C, WL+IEDW, shows off the short-lived 1939-style trainer markings on the otherwise plain RLM 63 finish. The presence of the fuselage cross on this enormous dive-bomber trainer dates the picture to about late 1939-1940. Unit is unknown.

46:    Junkers Ju 87A, B.604, was one of four used by the Hungarian Magyar Királyi Honvéd Légierő for dive-bomber training at Börgönd in 1944. Trainer status is indicated by the red code letters and the camouflage finish is RLM 70/71/65.

47:    Junkers Ju 87A, S13+S29, of an unidentified Stuka schule in the three-tone pre-war camouflage of 61/62/63. The 'S13' code is something of a mystery as this is usually accepted as identifying the parent Luftkreis, but there were never more than seven of these. It may simply be that the letter 'S' was added to the earlier operational unit code, the last part of which has been overpainted by '29'.

48:    Junkers Ju 87B, L1+AU, of 10./LG 1, in the standard dive-bomber markings and RLM 70/71/65 camouflage of the early war years.

Page 50

49:    Junkers F13, TV+OO, enjoyed a remarkably long life. This is, in fact, the much-modified first prototype, Werk Nummer 531, 'Nachtigall' – Nightingale – which survived from 1919! It is shown here in service with A/B 1 at Görlitz in summer 1940 in weathered metal finish with later Luftwaffe markings over the original D-1 registration, the lighter patch showing where this has been removed. At least five other F-13s are known to have worn Luftwaffe markings: BB+HG, BB+HU, GD+NS, NF+NY and TA+??.

50:    Junkers W34hi, TK+BN, of FFS (C) 13 at Roth-Kiliansdorf in July 1943. Uppersurfaces are overall RLM 70 Dunkelgrün.

51:    Junkers W34hi, BB+HC, in overall RLM 63, probably in service with FFS (C) 16. Not visible in this view are the non-standard upperwing crosses which were the same as those underneath.

52:    Junkers W34hau, DB+ET, Werk Nummer 3047, of A/B 32 at Pardubitz. The function of the small number '4' is unknown. Finish is RLM 70/71/65.

53:    Messerschmitt Bf 110G2/R-3, DT+NR, Werk Nummer 420012, once in service with BFS 8 as a blind-flying trainer, although it appears to have retained its armament.

Page 51

54:    Junkers W34hau, KV+AK, shows off its striking yellow codes which were repeated on the leading edges of the wings, a not uncommon practice in A/B 121 (based at Straubing) to which it belonged. The original picture shows a very dark finish, interpreted here as RLM 70. The unit badge has been recorded as having both white and red(?) backgrounds to the shield.

55:    Junkers W33he, DK+AM, is shown in overall RLM 02 when it was serving with A/B 32 at Pardubitz in December 1941.

56:    Heinkel He 70G, NV+BT, of A/B 113, Detmold, shows off its modified factory finish which has had the rear portion of the black fuselage flash overpainted RLM 02 to allow the call sign to be applied. The factory-applied lightning flash is often shown incorrectly in white, whereas close study of original photographs shows that it was in fact RLM 02 Grüngrau, the same as the overall finish.

57:    Heinkel He 70F, S4+Q22, wears highly unusual white codes on both the fuselage and underwing and large areas of yellow under the wings. There is a small Werk Nummer (possibly 1774) on the fin tip. Apart from the fact that the aircraft was in training school service in Luftkreis IV, probably in 1939, nothing is known of the machine. See photo 68.

58:    A rare Junkers Ju 160, PF+GC, of A/B 14 at Klagenfurt. Under the thin overspray of RLM 02 the original DLH registration, D-UFAL, and the name 'Jaguar' can still be seen.

Page 52

59:    Caudron C445, KI+WW, is a more colourful example than most of its kind in Luftwaffe service. Finished overall silver with a black anti-glare panel, the aircraft is believed to have belonged to Stab. Lfl. Kdo. 'Götterbote', hence the green band. It sustained minor damage after a forced landing by Leutnant Ruppel fifteen minutes into a test flight from Insterburg, East Prussia, on 24 June 1941.

Table 19

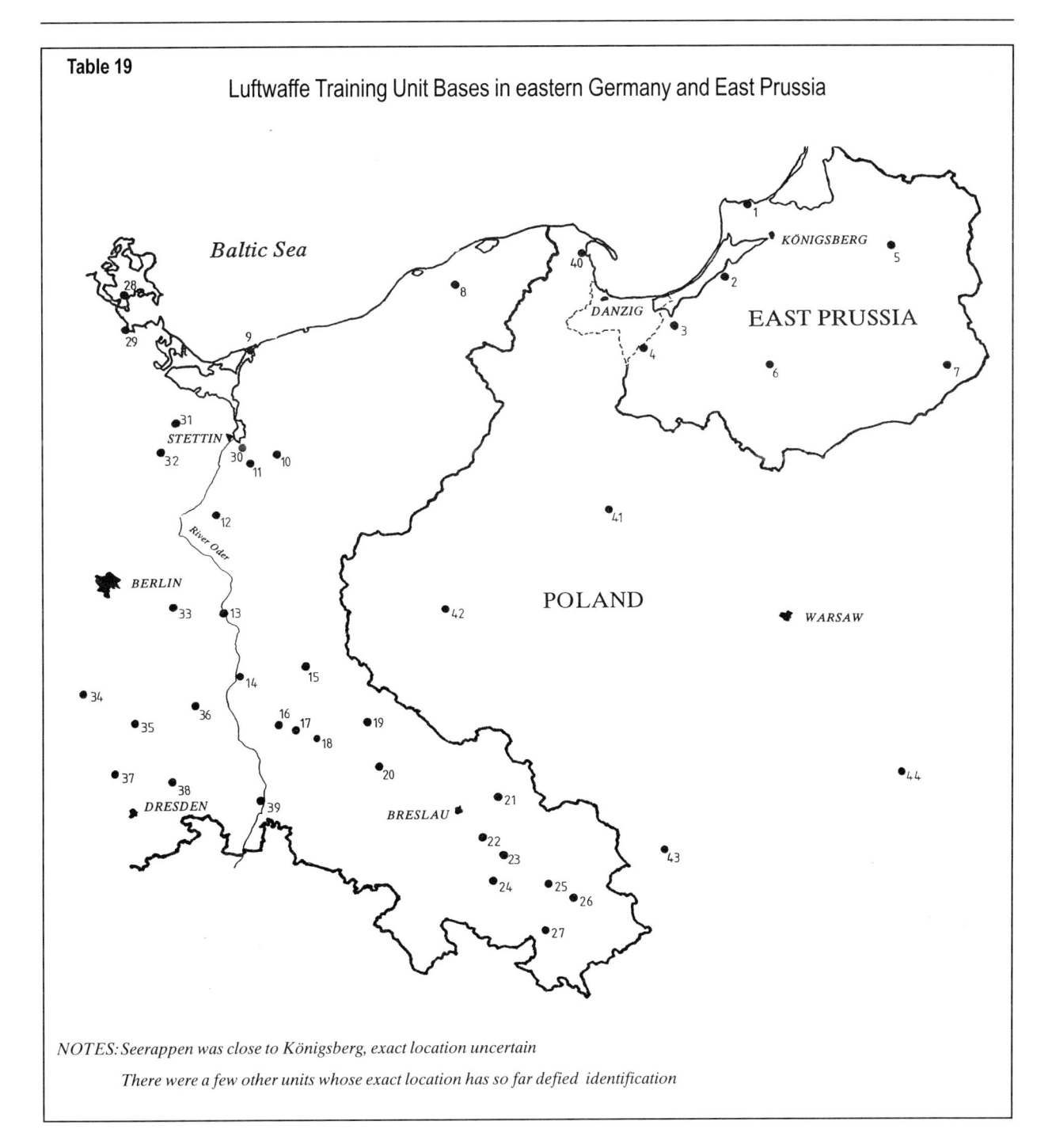

Luftwaffe Training Unit Bases in eastern Germany and East Prussia

NOTES: Seerappen was close to Königsberg, exact location uncertain

There were a few other units whose exact location has so far defied identification

1:	Neukuhren	16:	Sorau	31:	Pasewalk
2:	Heiligenbeil	17:	Sagan	32:	Prenzlau
3:	Elbing	18:	Sprottau	33:	Fürstenwalde
4:	Marienburg	19:	Glogau	34:	Brandis
5:	Insterburg	20:	Lüben	35:	Finsterwalde
6:	Allenstein	21:	Oels	36:	Cottbus
7:	Lyck	22:	Ohlau	37:	Grossenhain
8:	Stolp	23:	Brieg	38:	Kamenz
9:	Dievenow	24:	Grottkau	39:	Görlitz
10:	Stargard	25:	Oppeln	40:	Putzig/Rahmel
11:	Neumark	26:	Stubendorf	41:	Thorn
12:	Königsberg	27:	Gleiwitz	42:	Posen
13:	Frankfurt am Oder	28:	Garz	43:	Tschenstochau
14:	Guben	29:	Greifswald	44:	Deblin
15:	Rothenburg	30:	Altdamm		

60: Siebel Si 204D, BN+SE, wearing the typical RLM 70/71/65 finish for this type. White '8' was in service with FFS (C) 5 in early 1944, flying from Neubrandenburg. Normally black, the eagle in the unit emblem may have been red in this case.

61: Siebel Si 204A, EJ+XD, once served with FFS (C) 8, whose clover leaf emblem can be seen on the nose.

Page 53

62: Focke-Wulf Fw 58C, DK+FF, wears an odd camouflage scheme of RLM 02 grey overall with dark green, probably RLM 71, over the spine of the fuselage, the nose and on wing uppersurfaces. Almost certainly from FFS A/B 8 in 1940/41, then at Vilseck, the aircraft could be in service with LKS 7, which operated a very similar machine coded DK+FE.

63: A Czech Aero A304, VB+HU, of A/B 71 based at Prossnitz, Moravia. Originally a light bomber, all armament, including a dorsal turret, was removed for use in the training role. The aircraft wears a very loose and weathered pattern of two greens, probably RLM 70 and 71 with 65 undersides.

64: Junkers Ju 88A-10 Trop, L1+LW, Werk Nummer 8771, of 12./LG 1, wears the tropical camouflage scheme of RLM 78 Hellblau and RLM 79 Sandgelb, along with both yellow and white fuselage theatre bands. Seen here in North Africa sometime in 1941-42, the wingtips could be white or yellow, depending on whether the ground crew had had time to change the theatre markings after transfer from the southern Eastern Front.

Page 54

65: Junkers Ju 88A-12 in use as a blind-flying trainer with FFS (B) 34 at Kastrup, Copenhagen in Denmark between late 1943 until late 1944. Note that the aircraft has no underfuselage gondola.

66: Dornier Do 17E, BA+BF of FFS (B) 16 still retains its pre-war camouflage, but with the addition of generous areas of yellow to indicate its trainer status.

67: One of only two Heinkel He 111G-3 variants built with BMW radial engines (originally intended for Deutsche Lufthansa) CE+NX must have been one of the rarest aircraft in Luftwaffe training service. Helmut Rix flew this aircraft during his time in 1944 with FFS (B) 34 at Kastrup, Denmark, whose 'blind cow' emblem it bore on the nose.

Page 55

68: Heinkel He 42, D-ITUI, shows off the standard scheme for training floatplanes – all-silver with yellow floats. The aircraft is depicted as it appeared when in service with an unidentified FFS (See) and demonstrates the standard markings carried by the newly-emergent Luftwaffe in late 1935.

69: Heinkel He 42, WL+IFLU, of FFS (See) Pillau, still wears the standard trainer floatplane finish seen on D-ITUI, but wears the short-lived 1939-style trainer registration with a very cramped Balkenkreuze.

70: Overall RLM 02 Arado Ar 199V-2, NH+AM (originally registered D-ISBC) was one of only two prototypes of this light floatplane trainer built. The aircraft were found to be superfluous to requirements, but both served in their intended role with the Luftwaffe. This one spent some time in Finland before being shot down by the RAF off the Norwegian coast in 1943.

71: The Fieseler Fi 156 Storch was an unusual type in Luftwaffe training service. GA+TZ wears the usual RLM 70/71/65 camouflage and the seahorse emblem of A/B 5, sometime in 1940-41. It probably served as a communications hack with the instructors.

Page 56 (1/144 scale)

72: Junkers Ju 52/3mg4e, SE+HU, Werk Nummer 6132, was officially on the strength of FFS (C) 8 at Wiener-Neustadt, but like so many other training aircraft found itself pressed into service as a transport during the invasion of Norway in April 1940. On April 14, it forcelanded at Siverbo in Sweden after getting lost and had to be dismantled and moved to larger field for re-assembly. It eventually returned to Germany on 2 September. The black undersides are most uncommon on a Ju 52.

73: Dornier Do 23G, G.203, was one of three to serve as trainers with the Hungarian air force. Originally intended for use as bombers, the MKHL found the type no more satisfactory as a bomber than did the Luftwaffe, consequently, like the German versions, they were soon relegated to training. Shown here in markings used until March 1942, the aircraft was finished in a soft mottle, probably using Italian paints.

74: Once in service with Hansa Luftdienst, whose eagle emblem is still visible, this Messerschmitt M20b, WL-UKUM, was a very rare bird in Luftwaffe service. First entering service in 1931, this aircraft, Werk Nummer 542, was originally registered D-2025. Re-registered D-UKUM and named 'Westerwald' in 1933, in 1939 it acquired the WL-trainer code as shown here. The rudder and fin have been overpainted, possibly in yellow, but the red stripe behind the swastika still shows through. The aircraft was destroyed in 1942.

75: Junkers Ju 86E, TO+CV, Werk Nummer 198 was used as an advanced trainer by FFS (B) 16. Finish is RLM 70/71/65 with areas of yellow to indicate trainer status.

Inside rear cover

76: Gotha Go 145, H4+VA, Werk Nummer 1455, forcelanded at Basle in Switzerland on 30 November 1941. Flown by Gefreiter Lange, the aircraft was in service with the Stab/Luftlandgeschwader 1, a glider unit. Finish was described as steel blue, interpreted to mean RLM 76, with yellow 04 areas under the wing. The individual aircraft letter 'V' was in green.

77: Arado Ar 76, DA+BN, Werk Nummer 112, was flown by Unteroffizier Bruno Pacher during his time with A/B 23 at Baltringen in early 1942. Finish was overall RLM 63 or 02.

𝔙erleihungsurkunde

Ich verleihe dem

Unteroffizier Philipp Segeth

das Abzeichen für

Fliegerschützen

Berlin, den 5.Oktober 1940

Der Reichsminister der Luftfahrt
und Oberbefehlshaber der Luftwaffe
J. A.:
Der Chef des Luftwaffenpersonalamts

Nr. 45 961 /40   Generalleutnant

The award certificate for the air-gunner's badge given to Unteroffizier Philipp Segeth. Although the facsimile signature is that of Albert Kesselring, the award was actually issued over the initials of the unnamed Generalleutnant. All Luftwaffe aircrew qualification certificates were similar to this, only the type of qualification and the signature changing. The badge is a replica of that of an observer.

Extract from the logbook of Hans-Joachim Kalläne, a navigator with I./LLG 2, a glider tug unit. These show a few of his flights with BFS 4 at Wien-Aspern in September-October 1940. Aircraft used include Ju 52/3m, Ju 86 and He 111. Note how the Ju 52s still retain the 'G6' code of KGrzbV 104, a clear indication that their use as trainers was likely to be temporary at best.